MICHI SAAGIIG NISHNAABEG: THIS IS OUR TERRITORY

ARP Books (Arbeiter Ring Publishing)
205-70 Arthur Street
Winnipeg, Manitoba
Treaty 1 Territory and Historic Métis Nation Homeland
Canada R3B 1G7
arpbooks.org

Book design and layout by Relish New Brand Experience.
Cover image *Manoominike Mazina'anang* copyright © Elizabeth LaPensée
Title page image *Canoe Harvest* by Larry Jamieson, courtesy of Historic
Resources Branch of Manitoba Sport, Culture and Heritage

Printed and bound in Canada by Friesens on paper made from 100% recycled
post-consumer waste.

Second printing, January 2019

ARP Books acknowledges the generous support of the Manitoba Arts Council
and the Canada Council for the Arts for our publishing program. We acknowledge
the financial support of the Government of Canada through the Canada Book
Fund and the Province of Manitoba through the Book Publishing Tax Credit
and the Book Publisher Marketing Assistance Program of Manitoba Culture,
Heritage, and Tourism.

LIBRARY AND ARCHIVES CANADA CATALOGUING IN PUBLICATION

Williams, Doug, 1942-, author
    Michi saagiig nishnaabeg : this is our territory / Gidigaa Migizi
(Doug Williams).

Issued in print and electronic formats.
ISBN 978-1-927886-09-0 (softcover).--ISBN 978-1-927886-10-6 (ebook)

    1. Ojibwa Indians--History. I. Title.

E99.C6W55 2018   971.004'97333   C2018-901213-7
                                           C2018-901214-5

MICHI SAAGIIG NISHNAABEG: THIS IS OUR TERRITORY

Doug Williams (Gidigaa Migizi)

ARP BOOKS   WINNIPEG, MB

LEFT TO RIGHT: Madden Taylor was my grandmother's brother. He was born around 1895 and died in 1986. Beside him is James Makoons Taylor. He was born around 1875 and died in 1975. These were the ones I spent much of my childhood with on the land. Both of these men never went to school but they knew their oral history. Their stories came from their Elders from the 1700s. I dedicate this book to them.

CONTENTS

Foreword

LEANNE BETASAMOSAKE SIMPSON

Like many Indigenous people in Canada, I was born into the violent processes of dispossession and erasure, into a family that was located outside of our territory, and with little means to expose me to the rich intelligence of my mom's people, the Michi Saagig Nishnaabeg. This was a loss I was unwilling to live with, and so in my early twenties, I began a life-long practice of reconnection that is still very much in progress, but led me to in my mind, one of the most important Michi Saagiig Nishnaabeg intellectuals my nation has, Doug Williams.

Doug is a widely respected Elder, historian, hunter, fisher, ceremonial leader, language keeper and storyteller, past Chief and at times an activist. He is a prominent leader in the urban community of Peterborough, Ontario, in Curve Lake First Nation and throughout the Nishnaabeg nation. He has tremendous influence in the field of Indigenous Studies, and has been directly involved in the training of now over ten years of Indigenous academics through his position as Director of Studies in the PhD program in Indigenous Studies at Trent University. And while any one of these reasons is more than enough for a young Nishnaabeg to move home to learn from him, the thing that drew me to him was a gentleness I'd almost exclusively seen in the generation of Elders that came before him, and a profound ability to think inside the Michi Saagiig Nishnaabeg intelligence system. He not only embodies our governance and our political systems he thinks deeply about the underlying philosophies, theories and concepts that animate them. Combined with a sharp and decolonial political analysis, there is no one that has influenced, mentored and nurtured my own intellectual, political, and ceremonial life more as an Nishnaabekwe.

I started to attend Doug's talks and workshops when I moved back to Peterborough. This led to deeper conversations and visits, which led to ceremony. This in turn, turned into storytelling and then sugaring, ricing, fishing, medicine gathering and hunting, all the while, Doug patiently answering my questions about Nishnaabeg philosophy, political culture, conceptual thinking, and values. Each year we walked through the seasons on our land together, my thinking deepened. Each year we became better friends.

A decade passed. I knew more about Doug and his early life as we talked about the concepts that would inform my writing on treaties, governance, and resurgence. I was often blown away and inspired by Doug's historical knowledge, because it was unlike anything I had ever read. I came to understand this as a rare pocket of our oral traditions that often extended back to the mid 1700s. Two of Doug's uncles figured prominently in his stories, and these were very much *his* stories, Madden and Makoons.

Much of Doug's historical knowledge comes from "hanging around" with Madden and Makoons as a kid. Madden had been exceptionally good at escaping the clutches of the truant officer at school, and as such, had hung around with his own uncles, absorbing a Michi Saagiig Nishnaabeg way of being that has been under intense attack for the last 200 years. In a sense, this is where Doug's knowledge comes from, the resistance of a small child escaping the state run school system. This is where some the knowledge I carry comes from, a critical act of resistance and the successive committed acts of resurgence.

When Doug turned seventy years old, it became important to him to write down some aspects of the knowledge he carries. He wanted to make sure that the coming generations had a record of Michi Saagiig Nishnaabeg land tenure because this is so readily erased in present day southern Ontario, the ways we had been dispossessed of territory, the beautiful hidden resistance of our old people, as they inherit the responsibility to protect our lands for ones that are not yet born.

This book represents a very small fraction of what Doug knows and embodies. We have specifically focused on a Michi Saagiig Nishnaabeg political history that until this point, has only existed in the oral tradition, where it belongs. This book is a deliberate strategy to document from the perspective of one elder, what has happened to our people from the establishment of the reserve at Curve Lake, to early treaty negotiations, our relationship with the other Indigenous nations, the war of 1812, and of course, the devastation of the 1923 Williams Treaty. These stories are more than just a chronicle of oral history. They document Michi Saagiig Nishnaabeg as provocateurs, strategists, connectors, agitators and intellectuals. They show that resistance and resurgence have always been part of us.

Some of the chapters begin as a series of transcribed recordings Doug did on various topics. Others were interviews and conversations the two of us had on the land. Three chapters were previously written and published by Doug. The Nishnaabemowin was transcribed phonetically with Doug dictating the spelling and noting that although he is fluent, he is not a language expert. There is some fluidity in these stories and these tellings—Doug tells slightly different versions at different times. Other elders carry different versions. This is part of the richness of oral practices. We chose to edit the work minimally because as I read the manuscript I could hear Doug's voice in my head. This is how he speaks and as one of our most gifted orators, it seemed appropriate to preserve his voice, because this body of work is his body's work, and a gift to all.

Introduction

DOUG WILLIAMS

This book is not a western academic work. It comes from within Nishnaabeg intellectual practices. It is born out of a lot of Nishnaabeg thought, remembering, storytelling, years of transfer-ring knowledge from generation to generation, and a long mentorship with two Elders who remembered into the 1700s.

I want to write this down because the Michi Saagiig Nishnaabeg side of the story is almost lost in terms of how the history of Ontario has been told by the mainstream historians of Ontario. I have always found it intriguing that there is a difference between oral stories and the academic telling of events. Because I am involved in the univer-sity and teach Indigenous Knowledge in the academy, I have thought a lot about this. Academics often view oral storytelling as a weak link to history. The disciplines at university that particularly deal with First Nations—archeology and history—are full of white men who interpret events in their own way without regard to our knowledge. Indigenous Knowledge is still not considered a valid form of know-ledge in many disciplines. There are political consequences for this, these beliefs hurt our people and hurt our relationship to our land. Our knowledge is just as important as western knowledge.

This is a timely book at a junction of commissions like the Royal Commission on Aboriginal People, the Ipperwash Inquiry, the Truth and Reconciliation Commission, the Missing and Murdered Indigenous Women Inquiry, where we hear a lot about the impact of colonialism on our people. These reports emphasize the importance of Indigenous Knowledge and our Elders. There is now becoming an openness on the part of governments to acknowledge that what we know is significant even in the courtroom.

This book is putting forward the importance of our knowledge. I try to catch the tone, the rhythm, and the spirit of those old stories. Old stories we believe are support by a Manidoo (spirit) that we call Dibaajimowag. To Nishnaabeg, stories are alive. That is why it is important to carry this on from one generation to the next. This is how we transfer knowledge.

Michi Saagiig Nishnaabeg Creation Story

We should begin with a retelling of our Michi Saagiig creation story, because origin stories are stories that hold our fundamental values and ways of being in the world. There are at least four creation stories and some Elders say there are seven. There are also many, many versions of each of these stories, and although they are never dramatically different from each other, I think it is important to note that there are different tellings of these stories by Elders and storytellers and unique versions in different areas of Nishnaabeg territory. This is the second time life was created.

A long time ago, way back in time, it was total darkness. There was nothing. At this time the Gzhwe Manidoo had a dream. In that dream, Gzhwe Manidoo saw the world that we know today. Gzhwe Manidoo saw the mountains, the plains, trees, the rocks, deserts, great rivers, animals, birds flying and Gzhwe Manidoo saw humans. The dream stuck with the Gzhwe Manidoo and Gzhwe Manidoo thought that it must come about—it must happen.

It is difficult to translate Gzhwe Manidoo into English because the English language tends to describe Gzhwe Manidoo as a he, but Gzhwe Manidoo is neither man or woman, there is no gender and it is important to remember that is the way we describe things in Nishnaabemowin. That is a big distinction, and it is important to remember when we are telling the story in English. Gzhwe Manidoo is the one that loves us unconditionally. They are the one that we sometimes call creator, but Gzhwe Manidoo is really a benevolent spirit that accepts our most naked truths and loves us anyway.

The earth happened and everything was created instantly and everything was beautiful. This went on for a long time. Everybody was getting along in Nishnaabemowin we call it kina-bimaadiziwin. It was harmonious. It was an ideal environment. Everyone was kind. Everyone lived in peace with each other, including the animals.

That continued, until one day things started to go bad, they started to go wrong. Things did not work out. Everything died off, and nobody knows why that happened. It could be that life is actually not that easy to keep. Gzhwe Manidoo wanted us to be so good that when things started to happen even with the Gzhwe Manidoo's creation something went wrong. Everything died off. A few things were saved. Apparently the elements were saved. There was still the sun, the great waters, the land, but everything living had died off. This bothered Gzhwe Manidoo. Gzhwe Manidoo was upset.

The spirits that lived in the sky, went to Gzhwe Manidoo and asked if they could help. They knew Gzhwe Manidoo was feeling badly because the place they created has gotten into trouble. So Gzhwe Manidoo asked one of the beings to go down and see if creation could be fixed. That spirit's name was Gizhiigokwe, which means Sky Woman. Gizhiigokwe decided to come to earth and find a spirit partner. We are not exactly sure who that partner was, because she asked Gzhwe Manidoo for a partner so that they could create humans. Other animals were also involved in helping her create humans. She came from the Sky. The Haudenosaunee also have this story about a spirit that comes from the Sky. We were peacekeepers and we travelled all over north eastern North America sharing our versions of the story.

Gizhiigokwe came to try and create humans. The first time she tried, they died off. She had two kids, and they died. Something was not working right for the Gzhwe Manidoo's dream. It didn't come together. Gizhiigokwe went back to the Spirit World and told the Gzhwe Manidoo that she tried but that it didn't work out.

Another thing that happened at this point was a great flood. Things were happening physically on earth. The great flood changed the physical surface of the earth.

Gzhwe Manidoo told Gizhiigokwe to not give up and to keep trying to make Gzhwe Manidoo's dream a reality. Gizhiigokwe went back to earth. One of the animals from the first creation was the Turtle because it could live in the water. When the flood happened only the fish and the water animals like the beaver survived because they could swim. When Gizhiigokwe came down again, it was all water. Gizhiigokwe couldn't settle anywhere because she couldn't swim. Water was a strange element to her because she is from the sky. The turtle came to her and offered her a place to land on the turtle's back. The turtle is called Chi'mikinak, like the place in northern Michigan (Mackinak). We call this place Chi'Mikinak—the Great Turtle. Gizhiigokwe noticed all the beautiful designs on the turtle's back and from there came the thirteen moons as depicted on the turtle's back. The twenty-eight days for each moon are depicted around the rim. Gizhiigokwe ran her finger around the rim and thought that it had meaning. She thought the turtle must be carrying something. The turtle was and wanted to help her create the world again. I remember how beautiful it used to be. The turtle thought they needed to get some soil to make it happen.

Gizhiigokwe was sitting on Chi'Mikinak's back and all the water animals were watching. A bird that could swim and float, the loon had survived and offered to dive to the bottom to get the earth to put on the Chi'Mikinak's back—because of the teachings on Chi'Mikinak's back the earth will grow into the Great Turtle. The loon was gone a long time. Finally, loon floated to the surface, but it had drowned. Loon tried so hard, it had died trying.

The next day, Otter came to her and offered to dive down. The same thing happened and Otter floated up dead with nothing.

Then beaver offered to try and go further than the Otter and the Loon. The same thing happened, it floated up dead with nothing, even though the Gzhwe Manidoo gave beaver a special gift of being able to hold oxygen in its tail. That is why the tail of a beaver is so large. This time, it didn't help.

Gizhiigokwe was pretty disappointed. She was getting worried she may not be able to help Gzhwe Manidoo with the visions.

Muskrat came along and Gizhiigokwe told Muskrat what happened. Muskrat offered to dive because muskrats can also keep oxygen in their tails. So the Muskrat dove and was gone for what seemed like days. Gizhiigokwe and Turtle waited. Finally, Muskrat floated to the surface drowned, but clutched in Muskrat's paws was a tiny paw full of earth. They took that earth and put it on the Turtle's back as it was prophesized and thought out in the dream of the Gzhwe Manidoo. Sure enough that little bit of earth grew and began to have mountains, streams and lakes, as we know it today. Nishnaabeg country was created with beautiful big lakes. There were clouds, wind, rains, trees and beautiful animals—deer, moose, elk, caribou and bear were all created. Gizhiigokwe said I am going to go back and think about creating humans. Gizhiigokwe went back to the sky to contemplate. She went back and became the moon. Instead of calling the moon Dibi-giizis, which is night sun, we call her Kookoom or Nokomis or Chi'Nokomis. Nokomis said I am going to give the gift of giving birth to humans once they are created.

Gizhiigokwe then asked Gzhwe Manidoo for another spirit to help her create humans. Gzhwe Manidoo sent Pingizhimok (where the sun sets), the west. Pingizhimok is a spirit in male form and he picked a woman from earth. We do not know how the woman survived the flood. We don't know who that woman was. Maybe she was a spirit as well. One story says that Pingizhimok and this woman had two kids and the kids had a fight, and they killed each other. The essence was just not there. The second time, Pingizhimok picked another woman—Wenona. Pingizhimok and her tried again, and they had a boy and a girl. These were not a boy and a girl in terms of sexuality, but more in essence. They in turn had a child. That is how humans were created.

Madden & Makoons

When I was a kid, I spent a lot of time with Madden and James Taylor. I was raised by my Grandmother and Madden is her brother and he lived with us. He never married and lost his arm in a gun accident when he was thirty years old. I often say that I became his helper because he was shunned by the men as a hunting partner because of his disability. This meant that we spent a lot of time together and because of this I learned the ways of the land, the ways of our culture and many stories. As he grew older, he would chum with the older men who would come out with us, and they would share more stories. He also hung around with this one older man by the name of Jim Taylor. He was about twenty years older than Madden. Madden was related to Jim and would have been born around 1895. James Makoons Taylor was a descendent of John Taylor, the son of George Taylor and he was about 20 years older than Madden, so he would have been born in about 1875. Everyone called him Jimkoons.

Madden and Jimkoons took me all over in the bush and told me a lot of stories about Michi Saagiig Nishnaabeg history. What that meant for me as a young child was that I was getting stories from both my Grandparents and my Great Grandparents generations. Much of the knowledge in this book, comes from them.

Madden and Jimkoons had houses on the reserve, but they lived on the land. In the spring, they would hunt muskrat. They always took a break in June because the mosquitoes were bad then. In July, they would camp out on Boyd Island or Chi'Minis/Big Island, Bald Lake or Bobcaygeon. They taught me a lot about the impacts of the

1923 treaty because they lived through it. They ate black tern eggs in the spring because they were so harassed by the game warden for fishing. The game warden used to hang out at Fox Island—he eventually learned all the bays to hide in around that island. They were so harassed all through the 1920s, 1930s and 1940s. By the time I was hanging around them in the 1940s and 1950s they were too old to out paddle the game warden. They had to resort to eating other things.

I spent all my time with Madden in the summers. We talked only in Anishinaabemowin (Ojibway). We would visit other camps of families living on the land. We would spend nights out at camps. I heard so many stories sitting by the fire and many of the stories that I tell here, came from those two guys. They were amazing. They knew all the history of the Nishnaabeg up and down the river systems throughout Ontario. They talked about such people as Mashkinoge like he lived yesterday. They also talked about Chief Maskwaaki who was a very flamboyant individual, and they even told me one time that he wasn't buried at Chief's Island on Lake Couchiching but on an island in Pigeon Lake. Now maybe, they were pulling my leg. They knew of his grave at Chief's Island, and they told me that he wasn't buried there, but on an island in Pigeon Lake. They also talked about old Chief Paudash, again a very flamboyant orator and negotiator. He is the Chief that led our people back into Ontario when they returned in the late 1700s. They talked about many things—spiritual things. They had great admiration but fear of the Midwewein priests that would come here from Parry Island.

Whenever we would go out on the land, Madden and Jimkoons wouldn't bring lunch. They would eat seagull eggs, loon eggs the odd time, those big black water snakes, frogs, porcupine, squirrels, muskrats and turtles.

Madden and Jimkoons were great believers in tobacco. They didn't make a big deal about it. They would just quietly put it down once a day or when there was stormy weather. When it would storm, we would lie under the canoe and they would smoke their pipes.

They talked about when the Jiiskaan, Shaking Tent ceremony came to Curve Lake a long time ago, but they didn't do formal ceremonies.

One of their friends, Tom Taylor married a woman from Christian Island who had some relatives who were Mide from Parry Island and they would come and visit. Being the boy that was hanging around these old men, I was their helper when they would come to visit. One time we were at the canoe races, which was a great event and people would come from all over and race canoes against each other. I was there one time when these two older Mide from Parry Island came to visit. We sat to one side. All the men sat in a circle were talking. I could tell by Madden's demeanor that he was uneasy and scared of them but yet he treated them very gently. He respected them and he knew they had a lot of abilities in terms of spiritual power. At one point, they asked me to get them some food— they wanted hot dogs and ginger ale. I started to run up to the little booth and got them all hot dogs and ginger ale. There must have been about 12 older men in their seventies or eighties. They called me gweziins, meaning little boy. We sat down and I finally got everyone all the food they wanted and one of the Mide priests was wrapping a hot dog bun around the end of his cane. He was sitting next to the water on a bank. He dipped his cane into the water with the hot dog bun on the end and pulled out a fish. Everyone stopped talking and looked at this. He slapped the fish back into the water and had a good belly laugh. The other Mide noticed everyone was paying attention to this and thought he could do better. So he did this without a hot dog bun, got a fish and slapped it into the water again. I'll never forget this. It put me in awe. I asked Madden after, how could that be? He didn't want to talk about it. He just said to me in Nishnaabeg, that the priests were magic.

Nokomis

I was raised in a situation where there was a lot of kids around and a lot of aunties, uncles and grandparents in a multi-family atmosphere—what sociologists call "extended" families as opposed to the "modern nuclear family" consisting of mom, dad, and kid/s.

I grew up being raised primarily by my Nokomis (grandmother) who was a matriarch and was born in Curve Lake in the 1890s.

She was very much caught in a world of change. She spoke our language very well and lived a lifestyle that was Michi Saagiig Nishnaabekwe but she also tried to adapt to the world of Canadian things. She had to navigate the change.

She married twice. Her first husband died when she was in her 30s and she had to raise the kids on her own for a while until she married again.

She was amazingly adept at canoeing, and basketry was her forte. She traded her baskets around the lakes. She also liked to clean and do domestic work so she worked as a housekeeper for many of the cottagers who came in the summer months to this area. She was also an amazing cook and would cook for the area fishing lodges.

Adding to all of this responsibility she had a political sense and as a leader she ran and got in as a Councillor for the Band and she was active in politics for a while. She could span both worlds quite well.

I remember many fond memories of picking blueberries with her, picking apples with her, and even going into the rice beds with her and shooting ducks. Then we would come home and make duck soup.

One time, we went odemin (strawberry) picking and left early in the morning when the dew was still on the grass in June. She said "Hope we don't meet up with a bear."

Well, we were in amongst the brush near some meadows and I was making sure I was right beside my grandmother because I was scared of makwa (the bear).

I was so intently picking berries when I forgot to keep track of where she was. I looked up and she was not there.

I panicked. I started yelling for her so she could hear me. I was scared and I felt so lost.

She was only over a knoll about 10 feet away from me picking berries. When I yelled she stood up and said "Oh my gosh keep quiet the bears will hear you!" I was so pleased to see her.

She always said if we come across a bear we have to speak to it in Anisinaabemowin (Ojibwa) because it is the only language they can understand. You can tell it to go away in the language ... but that is another story.

Making Baskets with Nokomis

Another fond memory I have of Nokomis (my grandmother) is of the many activities we did together, in particular making baskets and all of the undertakings that entailed.

Every year she expected me and her brother Madden to go into the swamplands and harvest baapaagigun (Black Ash trees) for her. We would fell the trees and carry those logs on our shoulders over to our canoes and carefully paddle across the lake with those trees in our canoes—it was not easy.

When we got the logs home we would pound on them and pound them into splints. This was called baapaakegehwin (pounding into splints). The annual growth rings will separate into splints when you pound this kind of tree. You use the splints to make baskets.

Nokomis was very well known for her basketry and would make any size, from small dainty baskets to huge hamper and laundry basket styles, all made out of wood. These were extremely durable and there must still be some around this area, especially amongst the cottagers.

I remember we would load up the canoes with baskets and I would go and help her trade and sell them to farmers, cottagers, and settlers. We would trade and paddle along the shores of Chemong Lake, Buckhorn Lake, Pigeon Lake, and Sturgeon Lake. She would knock on doors—she had her favourites.

I remember one time she got me out of bed, "We have to load the canoes. I want to go to Sturgeon Lake and Fenelon Falls tomorrow and we will spend the night in Bobcaygeon. Make sure you have blankets."

We started out about mid-morning and paddled to Bobcaygeon. It would take us until about 4pm to get there, but it was a casual paddle and we fished along the way. We got a bass in a bay at Gchi Minis (Big Island) and then we proceeded to the Taylor camp on the far end of Bobcaygeon Island.

There was always someone at this camp ready to greet travellers and offer a place to stay. Murney Taylor, a young, very handsome man about 25 years old, was the only one there looking after the camp. He had a 4-walled canvas tent set up. He was so happy to see us and he welcomed us so warmly. We had a wonderful meal of bass which we made into a stew.

Then I slept and I remember the wonderful aroma of cedar boughs that covered the ground under me while Nokomis and Murney told stories deep into the night.

Bright and early the next morning we headed out onto Sturgeon Lake. Nokomis would drop into places and sell and trade her baskets—mostly trade. We would get items like food and clothing. My grandmother was so happy.

We would end up in Fenelon Falls and we would get some candy and maybe a drink—go walking around downtown—she liked a store there.

Then we would go back, sleep at Bobcaygeon and get back to Curve Lake the following day. Oh what beautiful memories. Except when we would trade her baskets with this one couple who would always give us button-less clothes. I called them Mr. and Mrs. Buttons. Nokomis did not like that ... but that is another story.

Creation at Kinomaagewapkong

Our people used to paddle to Kinomaagewapkong, the Teaching Rocks (Peterborough Petroglyphs), by going up Jack's Creek. At the two-mile mark there are rapids. They would get out of the canoe and walk west. The path was marked with either with trees with axe marks on them or bent bushes, and if those bent bushes didn't die, they would grow into big trees with bends in them. When you come to Kinomaagewapkong that way, you approach from the top of a hill and you can see the white rock down below. The rock used to be very white. When I was a kid, I remember it being much, much lighter than it is now.

The first time I heard of that rock was from my step Grandfather Elwood Copaway. He went there with a group from Curve Lake that included Amos Johnson and Reg Muskrat. I remember when he came home he talked about the rock. He was amazed by them. I was seven or eight years old, so this must have been 1950.

I asked the old guys I hung around with, Madden and Makoons about the rock. They didn't go there that often, but they knew about them and they had been there. David Johnson tells an interesting story about Kinomaagewapkong. His great grandmother is the mother of Amos Johnson. Her name was Mary Johnson. According to David, Mary used to say that the people covered the rocks up with moss when they weren't visiting them. They would uncover the rocks when they were visiting them.

In those days, we had to be very, very careful with practicing our culture and our spirituality. We had to do it very subtly. We put a lot of tobacco down. People would have to sneak to Kinomaagewapkong so that the Christian Nishnaabeg and the missionaries didn't find out. My uncles, Madden and Makoons knew a lot of songs but they were too afraid to sing. Everyone was too afraid to sing because they were afraid of being heard. Madden's sister knew a lot of songs. Her name was Mary Jane Taylor (née Williams) but she would only sing when she was drunk because she was afraid.

Our people have had a continuous relationship with Kinomaagewapkong. It isn't something we forgot about and found. We always knew about it. We always visited it. It was a very important place for us because of our teachings.

I started to visit there as soon as I had a car to get there. I knew that place was special. It was a spiritual place. Those teachings were put into me by the old people. I gave a lot of credit to those old people who put tobacco down because their beliefs were so beautiful. It was a deep belief of spirit. It was intimate. I was drawn to this place spiritually. The old people told me the reasons that we go there is because the rock can talk Nishnaabemowin. If you visit the site, and listen to the rock and the water, you could ask it questions. The spirits would answer.

I must have first went there when I was about 17 years old. My mom and my step dad took me there. It was at this time that the Zhaganash (white people) had found out about the site and it was in the newspapers. We learned from Elwood how to get there. I started going there regularly in my early twenties when I could drive. I've never been by canoe. Elwood always went by canoe. I would burn sweet grass there, as we did in the old days, and leave some wiike (rat root) there. I would pray in my language. I talked to the rock and the water. I would ask it questions, like can you be clear with my name? My clan? I could hear it answer back, but only Bozhoo/Aaniin. The rest was too muffled to understand. This was frustrating. In those days, I got the feeling that the creek flowing under the rock was more important than the drawings, or Gii masinigaawok—the picture writing. We went there to talk to the spirits. This was a place of healing. This was one of the places of Creation.

Nonkomig Mandigog

The Nishnaabeg believe there are four ways we were created: the earth, the sky, the water and spontaneously. There are different creation stories for each of these mechanisms of creation. Kinomaagewapkong is one of the sites of our creation from the earth. There are Manidoog or spirits that live down in the earth and they were powerful. If you asked them in a good way with good thoughts and a good heart, they would help. These were the Kichi Mandigoog of the Nonkomig, or the underground. That word later got ruined by the missionaries to mean hell. But our old ones believed Nonkomig was another world where all kinds of Manidoog lived that helped create humans—snakes, turtles, skinks, earth forming worms and Manidooshensag—bugs, spiders and insects. Theses beings created humans from underneath the earth and we emerged at Kinomaagewapkong.

The Nonkomig Mandigo and the world of the Manidooshensag, the insects created the Nishnaabeg that came from the earth at Kinomaagewapkong. This is the home of birthing, of creation. This is the home of our sexual ideas and characteristics. We describe the sexual organs of the woman as the earth. Our word for vagina is akiden, and the word for earth is aki. This is because women are connected spiritually to the earth and creation is an everyday process. We are continuously recreating. The sexual organs of a man are Nishee'ow—a good thing with spiritual connections. There are lots of glyphs with akiden and nishee'ow shown in them. This is emphasized when creation happens from the earth. Our old people weren't ashamed about their sexuality. They laughed about it. They joked about it. They were open about it. They told stories about it. There were lots of great Nanibush stories about sex. We are so uptight about sex now, and we can't talk it about it at all in institutions.

The story of our creation from the sky is well known. The story of us being created out of water comes from struggle. Some beings came out of the ocean and tried to live on land. Some struggled to breathe air and fit into the land environment. They were astounded by what was here because it was so unlike what they were used to. Some could not cope and they went back to the water. Some stayed and gradually grew into full human beings.

The Ocean People

The beings that came out of the ocean were the ones that taught us about our clan system—the dodemag. They told us to use the animals and the ones that were already here as teachers because they could show us how to live in a good way. It is from these people that we learned the ability to be peaceful people. This is why the Gchi Michi Saagiig Nishnaabeg were messengers between nations and between communities on earth, as well as messengers of peace from the spirit world.

Boshkaaniniwag

There were also people created spontaneously, instant humans, the Boshkaaniniwag. They were created suddenly. They took on all kinds of different forms as they tried to get it together. It wasn't neat and tidy. They carried a lot of spiritual knowledge but not a lot of practical knowledge. That's where they had to rely on other Nishnaabeg and animals for help.

When we were out hunting, we'd come across odd people but they were strange. We were impressed by their ability to see into the future, to tell the past and to transform into other beings. They could also transform into very old people or very young people.

These are the stories I think about when I go to Kinomaagewapkong.

The Building

We lost control of all crown land north of Curve Lake in the 1923 Williams Treaty. That is when Kinomaagewapkong got made into a Crown Game Reserve and then a provincial park. We have always had some influence over how they managed the park—we refused to let them build camp sites, we negotiated for control for the gate and a certain percentage of the gate fees, we refused to allow a restaurant and huge interpretive centre to be built. Merrit Taylor and I both have keys to the site. We've never had the resources to protect the site from vandalism, but this is our land and our site.

In 1985, without consulting with the Elders and traditional people, the provincial park people built a building over the site. It breaks my heart. The rock now can't feel the rain or the snow. They filled the creek with concrete so we can no longer talk to the spirits. They put cement over some of the glyphs so you can't see them now. This is heartbreaking. It is sacrilegious. It is insensitive. They need to fix these problems. The roof needs to be open. They need to remove the concrete and cement. They need to make us a ceremonial spot where we can fast and have ceremonies and not be bothered by tourists. This is not a tourist site it is a sacred site.

Our old people told me that there are four sacred sites between the Ottawa River and Niagara Falls along a north eastern direction. Kinomaagewapkong is one of them. There is one west of Kinomaagewapkong and this is a geyser—a place where steam came out of the earth and the spirits would speak with us. It was prophesized that this would close up when the white people came. I think it did. No one knows where it is now. There are also two spots north east towards the Ottawa River. I'm not sure where these are, but I would guess that one is The Gut, and the other is Mazinaw Lake.

Kina Gchi Nishnaabeg Ogaming

According to Michi Saagiig Nishnaabeg oral traditions, southern Ontario, particularly the area west of Gananoque and to Long Point on Lake Erie, along the north shore of Lake Ontario and all its tributaries and rivers that drain into it, is the territory of the Michi Saagiig Nishnaabeg. This has always been true. Our territory of the Michi Saagiig Nishnaabeg is the north shore of Lake Ontario stretching from where the St. Lawrence River at the eastern end of Lake Ontario and the territory stretches to the west to approximately Niagara Falls. We are river mouth people that lived at nearly every river that flowed into Lake Ontario. Starting in the east this would be the Rideau River, the Moira River, The Trent River, the Ganaraska River, Wilmot Creek, Rouge River, Don River, Etobicoke River, Credit River, Sixteen Mile Creek, and Burlington Bay as it is known today. The reason that we are here is because we love this territory. Our stories go back to the ice ages when Nishnaabeg moved into this area and the ice was still here. The Michi Saagiig Nishnaabeg lived here and they were traditionally the people that fished the Atlantic Salmon that came up the St. Lawrence River and spawned in the great rivers that flowed into Lake Ontario. Our people remember those days. Salmon were our staple. We enjoyed this good life, being sustained by the salmon.

The Aayadowaad (Huron) also lived amongst us with our permission. They moved into our area around 1000 AD and some archeologists even say as early as 600 AD but we remember them coming from the south. They had permission to come to our traditional territory by the Michi Saagiig Nishnaabeg and the Odawa

Nishnaabeg. The Odawa were more numerous at this time and they backed up the Michi Saagiig Nishnaabeg if there was any trouble. We intermarried quite a bit. The Aayadowaad got permission to come here and live on the north side of the lake. Before that they lived south of Niagara. They lived in the fields that were there empty because the Nishnaabeg were living on the rivers and the river mouths. We were the shoreline people and they were the agricultural, field, gardening people. We lived quite nicely like that for some time. We were symbiotic. We traded with Aayadowaad, especially in the winter. We traded fish and animals. They had crops—corn, beans, squash and vegetables, lived in villages and stored food. It is said later that the Aayadowaad asked to move further north to Lake Simcoe. The Odawa along with the Michi Saagiig Nishnaabeg said yes. They were bringing their friends the Neutrals, tobacco growers and the Petun.

The Michi Saagiig Nishnaabeg are part of the greater Nishnaabeg nation but at the same time we are also a distinct group that made many agreements with the Canadian or British governments. In our language, Michi Saagiig Nishnaabeg means the people that live at the mouths of rivers. It is not a settler term. It comes from our language. It is how we refer to ourselves and how other Nishnaabeg refer to us. Michi Saagiig Nishnaabeg is used to describe our people in the notes on the Treaty of 1701 in Montreal, and it appears on a map done by British cartographers in the 1700s. It is also used in the journals of the Jesuits.

Michi Saagiig Nishnaabeg travelled extensively in our homeland. We moved around according to the seasons. We did not colonize and settle areas like the French and British. They found it difficult to understand how we occupied our territory. They found it difficult to mark us on their maps because we were always moving. We travelled all through the Great Lakes especially during the summertime where we would go from Fort Albany to the east and up and down the St. Lawrence River. We traded in Montreal. We went as far as Sault Ste. Marie, down into Michigan and around in Lake Huron or Odawa Gaming or Aayadowaad Gaming and over to Lake Erie. We spent time on Gichi Ziibi, the St. Lawrence River. We were good paddlers and we made excellent canoes. Two people paddling in the summer could reach 100 miles. It was no big feat to go to Parry Island in a couple of days and Sault Ste. Marie in four days. We intermarried with the Chippewa'ag Nishnaabeg. Chief Miskwaky, (Maskwaaki) also identified as Michi Saagiig Nishnaabeg, because his mother was Michi Saagiig Nishnaabeg from the Rice Lake area. We identified ourselves as Michi Saagiig Nishnaabeg. That is an adjective. When you use it alone you should correctly say Missisaagiig or Michi Saagiig as a plural noun.

As I've said before, the Michi Saagiig Nishnaabeg have been here in Ontario for a long, long, time and are descendants of the people that were living here in the time of glaciation, 8,000 years ago and beyond. As Nishnaabeg we tell the stories that we were here, temporarily leaving at times because of weather, severe glaciation and diseases, and the expansive ideas of other nations who were being prompted by the colonizers. We have loved and cherished this land for a long, long time.

Michi Saagiig Nishnaabeg History

When I was driving into town this morning along River Road, I was remembering that we call December, Kitchi Gisinaa-Giizis, cold month. When the missionaries came, they changed it to Manidooo-Giizis, Spirit Moon to reflect their beliefs, not ours. November was Aazhaagadin-Giizis, the moon when the ice crosses the lake. January was called Maaji Giizis, the first moon. It's always interesting to me the way our people used to name the seasons and mark time. We used to say Shkwaamaagee Giizis—meaning "no more movement" or "the end of movement" or "the sun is now standing still. It is not going anywhere." Our old people used to choose a tree as a marker. They would watch the sun. Line it up with the marker. When the sun was still going south, zhaawenong. It stops, then it comes back. Nike zhaw miinawaa. Right now, it is standing still in December. It doesn't move very much. This is what we now call solstice. Starting about January 15, you'll start to notice the sun comes back, but before that for about 3 weeks, it stands still. We used to mark this time of year Kitchi Gisinaa Giizis by feasting, having ceremony and celebrating. All Indigenous peoples throughout the world celebrate it this time of year. For Nishnaabeg, solstice means standing still.

I want to talk a little bit now about Michi Saagiig Nishnaabeg history. The ones that think they are smart from the university say that we came to this part of Ontario 9,500 years ago. That's a long time. Rice Lake, Pamitaashkodeyong, which means "where it burns and where it travels" because our people used to burn the south shore of Rice Lake to maintain a mishkode—a meadow or a prairie. We had prairies all over the place in those days. Archaeologists, the ones that suffer from the disease of archaeology, say they have evidence that paleo-Nishnaabeg hunted caribou around Rice Lake. Our Michi Saagiig Nishnaabeg oral traditions tell us that there were caribou here all over the place. For most of central Ontario, the Dodem that is strong is mainly atik—the caribou. Curve Lake is the only one in all of Nishnaabeg country that call a cow, atik. All other Nishnaabeg call a cow is bizhiki, which is buffalo. Our claim to fame is that we call the cow, caribou and if you are crazy we say giiwenaadis which means "your head is twirling on your shoulder". Any other Nishnaabeg would say, "you are half there".

Susan Jamieson, an archaeologist from Trent, and Kris Nahrgang from Burley Falls, came up with a site at Burley Falls which they dated as 12,000 years ago. They fight amongst themselves as to whether or not that is true. They argue if they got the date right, if they sent it to the right lab. To me, it doesn't really matter. I'll show you the way I see it.

Nishnaabeg believe we were created here long before this. I already shared our creation stories with you in the previous chapters.

It took billions of years to create life as we know it in four quadrants or stages. If the earth was created 1 billion years ago, then the Elements were created 250 million years ago, the Trees and Plants another 250 million years after that, and then the Animals 250 million years after that. Then they all helped humans to be created. The world existed for millions of years without humans. We were created last.

When we pray traditionally, we give miigwech (thanks) to all of this. Miigwech has an explanation. It is a gift giving. It comes from the root word for giving. Miigwe is the act of giving. That's where that word comes from. When you are given a gift you say "miigwech". We give thanks for all kinds of gifts, material and spiritual. People who are really good at this take a long time to do this—pray about elements, plants, animals and then Nishnaabeg. This is important because our oral history covers millions of years. There were four kinds of Nishnaabeg before modern Nishnaabeg; Misabe, Msnaabi, Nswinaabi, Niwiinaabi and then Nishinaabe. Nishnaabeg, like all peoples have changed through time. Our language has changed as well—now we use Naabi for husband but in the old days we used this as a human. In the old days, the old people used Nooka for bear, now we use Makwa.

Our creation stories tell us how we got here and how the world was made. I've told you the story about Gizhigookwe, Sky woman and the Kinomaagewapkong. Basil Johnston also has other ones in his work and so do the Mide. The Haudenosaunee know that, they have the Gizhigookwe story too. All of the northeastern Nishnaabeg had the story of Sky Woman. They say we were created at the mouth of the Great River, Kitchi Ziibi, which is known as the St. Lawrence River in English. Over time, and there is a lot of story in here, we got to Ontario.[1] Michi Saagiig Nishnaabeg also carry other creation stories. There are the ones I shared earlier form the Petroglyphs as well. All of our stories tell us that the Nishnaabeg were the first people in our territory.

Zhooniya Zaagiigan is Lake Simcoe. Nishnaabeg called Lake (Huron), Odawa Zaagiigan. We called Lake Ontario Chi'Nibiish. Ojibwe and Bodewadami (Potawatomi) people had their own territories. On the south shore of Lake Erie is where the Aayadowaad lived. The Neutrals were between Lake Ontario and Lake Erie. The Petun were tobacco planters over by Lake Aayadowaad. The Michi Saagiig Nishnaabeg were on the north shore of Lake Ontario right from Gananoque to Long Point on Lake Erie, and all the rivers that flow into Lake Ontario. The reason we are called Michi Saagiig Nishnaabeg is because we lived in the mouth of the rivers. At about 1000 AD or maybe earlier, the Aayadowaad (Huron) came into Ontario. That is when corn came into Ontario. The Three Fires Confederacy was made up of Ojibwe (Chippewa'ag, Michi Saagiig Nishnaabeg, Nipissing Nishnaabeg), Bodewadmi and Odawa Nishnaabeg.[2] The Aayadowaad came to the Three Fires Confederacy and asked for land. The Odawa Nishnaabeg were strong people. The Odawa Nishnaabeg said yes. The Michi Saagiig Nishnaabeg agreed. The Aayadowaad got to know the land and the rivers. There is lot of evidence of them because archaeologists like to study them, because it is easy. The Neutrals grew tobacco and corn. They were really amazing people according to the archaeologists—good palisades to protect them from the Nadaweg[3], beautiful long houses. The dividing line was the Niagara River. This is how it looked at the time of Champlain.

Our Friends, the Aayadowaad

The Aayadowaad were good friends and allies of the Nishnaabeg. The ones I used to talk to would call them Aayadowaad, almost sounds like Wendat. Aayadowaad means "the people who live in houses" in this instance it means "people who live in long houses." Aayadowaad came from the south according to the stories I was told as a young boy. They came here many, many years ago. In my own research, it has become apparent through archeological and geological study that the Aayandowaad have been in Ontario since approximately 800 AD. The corn pollen shows up in the study of soil around that time. This is consistent with our stories that the people from the south came around that time and they brought corn and they wanted to live with us, in our area. They wanted to live together with us. A big council was held and it was agreed by all Nishnaabeg in the surrounding area that included all of the Odawa Nishnaabeg and the Michi Saagiig Nishnaabeg and others. This group was manly led at that time by Odawa Nishnaabeg Chiefs. This is consistent with later stories told about the great achievements of War Chiefs like Ma'iingan and Pontiac and Mokomonish.

The Aayadowaad were very friendly to us. We knew their language and they knew ours. The Aayandowaad live agriculturally inland and the Michi Saagiig Nishnaabeg lived along the lakes and shorelines and at the river mouths. After so many years, according to the old story, again the Aayandowaad, along with the Neutrals and the Semaa'o'ninwag, or the Petun, meaning the tobacco people were really good friends with Ma'iingan. They asked again if they could move from the fields around the north shore of Lake Ontario to the area surrounding Lake Simcoe heading towards Georgian Bay. That was one of the homes of Ma'iingan and his people and also of the Beaver people. They were given permission around the year 1100 AD to move into this area. This is consistent with geological and archeological studies. The agreement was that the Michi Saagiig Nishnaabeg and the Odawa would let them live here. They had no sovereign rights and they had a meeting of the council of the Odawa Nishnaabeg and the Michi Saagiig Nishnaabeg and other Nishnaabeg that would prompt any changes to this agreement. The old people always said there was a wampum made to this effect, but this wampum has disappeared and to present day no one knows where it is located. A wampum is an agreement or a pact between individuals or nations. It is symbolized by beads that tell a story. The story is carried as long as the agreement remains alive. It should be told and retold on an annual basis.

These stories were told by several people, mainly the old people, my great uncle Madden and his friend Makoons who was twenty years older and also another friend of theirs.[4] My mother's cousin who is older than me who is the next generation up told me that we were relatives of Mashginozhe who was Michi Saagiig Nishnaabeg, Chippewa'ag and Odawa all in one. His sister married into the Odawa. His mother was also Odawa. His father was Chippewa'ag and Michi Saagiig Nishnaabeg.

Back to the Aayadowaad, I was told by Elders and stories handed down through Ma'iingan that the Aayadowaad were very friendly to us. We intermarried at times, but we mainly lived gifting each other with food. They would give us corn and squash and we would give them deer, fish, ducks, geese, and things of that nature. We got along for years and years before the Europeans came and disrupted this part of Ontario. We were able to fend off any trouble the Nadaweg (Mohawks) would give us from the south. The Aayadowaad were a well-organized nation and they had really nice homes. The stories speak also very highly of the Neutrals. It is said that when the Nishnaabeg went to visit the Neutrals, their houses were neat and tidy and their corn and tobacco was prized. They lived just west of Niagara Falls in Michi Saagiig Nishnaabeg territory.

The Aayandowaad were devastated by diseases, and they were upset by the Haudenosaunee, the Nadaweg. Some of them took refuge with us. Nearly all of the Petun[5] went to the Odawa Nishnaabeg and were looked after by the old Chiefs there like Ma'iingan. The Neutrals paid heavily for these diseases and were absorbed by the Nadaweg. The old people said that most of the Seneca around Niagara Falls were Neutrals that were absorbed by the Seneca. An interesting part of this is that the Erie People that lived on the south shore of Lake Erie and whom tattooed their bodies quite heavily were also absorbed by the Nadaweg. Our people used to say the Seneca were mostly "other people"—the Aayadowaad, the Neutral and the Petun. The Aayadowaad died very quickly and I remember the stories of bodies lying all over the place and our people would bury them or take them to islands to look after them, feast for them. Because we knew that they could not do the usual burials themselves because of how fast they were succumbing to the disease. Today, some of the remaining Aayadowaad assert their sovereignty over southern Ontario and over our territory. I am not sure if this is true but I have heard it from reliable sources. They are saying they have rights to this area without knowledge of the agreements that we had with them years ago. It is important to acknowledge these agreements. This is our territory and we let them come here to grow their corn. They stayed for a long time. We remained friends until the end.

There is an old Michi Saagiig Nishnaabeg story about our relationship with the Aayadowaad in the 1600s. The story says that a group of Michi Saagiig Nishnaabeg was travelling one down the Albany River, going to Fort Albany to trade. We preferred to go there to trade at that particular time with the English, instead of going to Montreal to trade with the French. We were going to Albany and some Aayadowaad were travelling with us. We also met up with some Mohawks and Onandagas, and they asked if we were all Michi Saagiig Nishnaabeg. We told them we had some Aayadowaad with us. They said they wanted the Aayadowaad because we are at war with them. As soon as that was said, a few of the Aayadowaad ran into the bush, and the Michi Saagiig Nishnaabeg told the Nadaweg you can't do that. We're friends. We are here to protect them. There was a lot of discussion and finally the Mohawks and the Onondagas left, and the Nishnaabeg went into the bush and got the Aayadowaad and we continued on together.

Samuel de Champlain

The colonial historical record that says that Mississauga people settled on the north shore of Lake Ontario in the mid-1700s. This is absolutely incorrect. Diamond Jenness, a well-known anthropologist and historian from the 1930s, has contributed to this misunderstanding. His book, *Indians of Canada* is recognized by the courts and by the government of Canada as being the official documentation of where our people lived throughout Canada. His work is very problematic for the Michi Saagiig Nishnaabeg. He got his information on us from the French and the Jesuits. The Jesuits were the ones than came upon the Michi Saagiig Nishnaabeg around the Mississauga River near Blind River in the 1600s. They documented this in their writings. Of course we were there. We travelled all over our territory. We were not settlers. We did not settle into villages. Our territory has always been the north shore of Lake Ontario and we moved all around that area.

Samuel de Champlain was the first European to reach our territory in 1615 when he travelled through our Nishnaabeg country. He was attracted more to the Aayadowaad than to the Michi Saagiig Nishnaabeg because the Aayadowaad lived in villages and the French could relate to that, while we lived in wigwams and could dismantle them and move quickly. He wasn't too interested in the Michi Saagiig Nishnaabeg because we were paddling around in canoes. The Aayadowaad guided Champlain through here—through Aayadowaad country and Lake Simcoe. The Talbot portage is now part of the Trent System, but it was a long portage over to Balsam Lake for the Nishnaabeg. Once you got to Chemong Lake, there was the Chemong portage that took you to Rice Lake. Then there was another portage from the east side of Rice Lake called the Percy Portage. The end of the Rice Lake had a portage over to Lake Ontario. There was a path to Scugog Lake. Then the big one from Toronto to Lake Simcoe. In the chronicles of Champlain, he only mentions the Aayadowaad, but actually we were here as the true "owners" of the land. We were given this land by the Gzhwe Manidoo.

Champlain came through our territory and he spent his first winter in Ontario in 1615-1616 with the Aayadowaad. This is important to remember because him and his men, including Étienne Brûlé, were travelling with viruses. They were carrying great sicknesses. The viruses were introduced into Aayadowaad country when they over wintered. Between 1620-1630, a large number of Aayadowaad died.

Champlain left and went back to Quebec, and then all the way back to France to marry the daughter of the King's secretary in France. After the marriage, Champlain came back and him and his men are full of viruses again. Champlain travels again in our territory—he was the first white man to tell about Niagara Falls and even to Superior. There are lots of stories told by the Nishnaabeg when the French started to come into the area and many relate to the diseases that were brought here by the French. It was Brûlé that came and spent the winter here amongst the Aayadowaad and the Michi Saagiig Nishnaabeg and apparently he went quite far—even as far as Lake Superior, guided by the Michi Saagiig Nishnaabeg/Odawa who could paddle from one end of the territory to the other in a couple of days. It wasn't unknown for them to go from here to the Toronto area, then Sault Ste. Marie in 4-5 days, even less if the weather was good and they paddled long days and short nights. In June, you could cover a lot of territory.

In the history books, you read that he was "discovering," but what he is actually doing is spreading viruses. Pretty soon, 40,000 Aayadowaad goes down to 7,000 people. The Neutrals are down to 800 people. They really suffered. The Erie people were devastated as well. We don't know how many people we lost but we know that Michi Saagiig Nishnaabeg are not affected to the same degree because we were not living in longhouses. We lived in small family groups and we travelled a lot. It is hard for a virus to catch up to people who are constantly moving around. In the meantime, we were all struggling with Nadaweg They were our traditional enemies but we have made a lot of treaty over time and now we get along beautifully.

The Nadaweg were not as infected by the viruses because Champlain and his men weren't travelling in their territory. The Nadaweg got 800 rifles from the British in the 13 Colonies, and when we saw that, we paddled away to the north. The first ones to be annihilated by diseases and rifles were the Neutral. By 1649, there were no Neutrals. By 1650 there were no Erie people. By 1653 there were only a few Aayadowaad left. The priest that was following Champlain around took some Aayadowaads over here and over here, to help them. By 1654 there is nobody in southern Ontario because they were either dead, or they had left because of the diseases. The Michi Saagiig oral traditions say that we left southern Ontario because of the diseases and we intended to come back to our territory once the diseases had subsided. Historians say that we came back because southern Ontario was abandoned by the Nadaweg and the Aayadowaad. That is not true. We were here before that, we left to escape the diseases and then we came home.

Remember, the Michi Saagiig Nishnaabeg were travellers. We were all over our territory. When the Jesuits saw us at the Mississauga River (near Blind River, Ontario), they assumed that was our village. We were not settlers. We were travellers. We were in the north for about ten years in the Mississauga River area to escape the diseases. We were temporarily in the Blind River area because Nishnaabeg were escaping the disease and the violence in the south. The old people always say we were gone away from fishing, from fishing the salmon, for about ten years. We loved to fish the salmon. We are the fishing people, and we came back because it was our home and we missed our Salmon relations. We were back in the southern parts of the territory by the end of the 1600s.

Michi Saagiig Nishnaabeg travelled. We visited. We went to Georgian Bay a lot. We married people from Georgian Bay. We moved a lot during the summertime. It is only logical that we would go to Georgian Bay during the time of diseases or when the Nadaweg were flexing their muscles south of us. We found ourselves around Manitoulin Island at the time the Jesuits were coming around. They documented into history us having that area as our homeland. I would like to make it clear that this is not my understanding. Our homeland is the north shore of Lake Ontario—from the Grand River in the west to Gananoque to the east. The misinformation Jenness introduced into the historical record is incorrect and we must correct it.

The Haudensoaunee have different stories about their territory. At this time, they claimed the Mohawk Valley, south of Lake Ontario, as their territory. When the Michi Saagiig Nishnaabeg decided to go back to our territory in the south, the Nadaweg were living in it and we had a very big conflict. Our great Chiefs, particularly Potash, tells the story of how we came down from the south, what is known today as the Trent Severn Waterway.

We got some help from Nishnaabeg from Georgian Bay, the Sault area and Manitoulin Island. Ma'iingan was a powerful Chief of the Beaver people, Amikwag. The Beaver people lived on the eastern side of Georgian Bay down towards the mouth of the Severn River. The Nipissings were another powerful people that lived along the French River and into Lake Nipissing, but all of these groups were Nishnaabeg and we knew them more by clans. We knew the Manitoulin Island people as the Fish people, and the Great Chief Shingwakoonse, was a very powerful Chief. There were also other Chiefs from Manitoulin and of course Pontiac from the Odawa Nishnaabeg had a lot of influence. The Nishnaabeg along with others from the bottom of Lake Aayadowaad (Huron) decided to come and push the Nadaweg back south. A number of Nishnaabeg gathered, old Potash told this story to his family and one of his grandsons told about it in a poem or a story that was written in 1925.[6] The group that was coming down to clear the Nadaweg out, eventually got to the narrows at Mnjikaning, the home of the Chief Maskwaaki and his partner, another Chief Nanigishkom where the fish fence is located.

Maskwaaki was a very well respected chief, along with the descendants of Ma'iingan, along with some Odawa, from Manitoulin Island with the Michi Saagiig Nishnaabeg headed by Potash and the great Chiefs like Ogimaa Binesi and Wabikinini and Chinibish from Chief Acheton (from Toronto portage area).

Maskwaaki was an Atik, a caribou, along came Assans (Little Clam) who was otter, Potash was crane, Ma'iingan was an Amik, and the people from Manitoulin, they told the Nadaweg to leave. Some of them resisted, Potash describes that, but you know, Nishnaabeg were pretty strong in all kinds of different ways. When they were having trouble with the Nadaweg in the late 1600s they gathered at a big meeting in Sault Ste. Marie. The Nadaweg were upset with us and now they have these rifles. So a decision was made. They are coming up here in the summers paddling their canoes and the Nishnaabeg waited for them in one time. Two thousand Nadaweg came up to Sault Ste. Marie to drive the Nishnaabeg further. The Nishnaabeg pushed back, killed them all except for one, and told the one to go back and tell the others not to come this way, because you will get real hurt. The Haudenosaunee remembered that, and they backed off from the Nishnaabeg. Once the Nishnaabeg got there, they acted together, nobody in North America could beat them. People feared Ma'iingan. They were guerilla type fighters.

There is a lot of conflict and misunderstanding between Michi Saagiig Nishnaabeg and other Indigenous nations about land in central and southern Ontario. There is a reason for this—colonialism. All Indigenous nations in the area have suffered because we have been dispossessed of our territories, because there has been so much settlement and development on top of us, and because of diseases. This is the root cause of our conflicts. We were all trying to survive.

I have written repeatedly in this book that I understand the north shore of Lake Ontario to be Michi Saagiig Nishnaabeg territory, and the south shore of the Lake, Nadawe territory. I have written my understandings about the agreements we made with the Huron to have their villages on our side of the lake. By the end of the 1600s all of these nations are feeling the impacts of colonialism—war, disease, displacement and encroachment. We are starting to fight each other over land, when the people we should be fighting are the British and the French.

We have a treaty and wampum with the Nadawe that they call the Dish With One Spoon, and it is a beautiful concept about sharing land and respecting the other's sovereignty. We made this treaty with Kanawake in Montreal in 1701. There were some misunderstandings though about this treaty. I understand that we made it with Kanawake, not all of the Nadawe. The rest of the Nadawe were not present at that meeting. So what our old Chiefs think has happened, is that when the British took over from the French in this part of the territory, the rest of the Nadawe went to the British and said we have a wampum agreement that we can hunt in the territory of the Michi Saagiig Nishnaabeg. The Chiefs think that naively the British may have agreed to this.

However, at a later meeting, with the Nadawe, it is recorded that in 1840 Maskwaaki Yellowhead, literally means "Red Earth," stood up and said several things to make it clear to the Nadawe that the Dish with One Spoon was only made with the Kanawake in 1701, and that it was no longer valid. The speech was recorded by an interpreter, that got it partly right. That at a certain point at The Narrows—which means at Couchiching (the narrows between Lake Couchiching and Lake Simcoe) that Our Fathers placed a dish with ladles around it. The ladles were the Six Nations, who said to the Nishnaabeg that the dish or bowl should never be empty. But Maskwaaki was sorry to say that it had already been accepted, not by the Six Nations residing at Grand River but with the Kanawake Nadawe residing near Montreal. That's a quote. This tells me even in writing and it is verified by Oral Tradition, that Dish with One Spoon's idea was only made with the Kanawake Nadawe.

Maskwaaki went over these duties and the responsibilities of these fires at the 1840 meeting. This is documented in the council minutes. There were a lot of Chiefs there—from St. Clair, Munsee, Saugeen, Cold Water, Lake Simcoe, Balsam Lake, Mud Lake, Rice Lake, Alderville, and Credit. At that meeting, they smoked the Pipe with the British Colonel. Six Nations were invited and were there, the Chief whose English name was Joseph Sawyer spoke to the council that was held at Credit River in around 1840 and he said that the meeting was called to renew the meeting of friendship which had been made by their forefathers, and the Six Nations Chiefs. He talked about the time when the hearts of their fathers were black towards each other and much blood was shed. He went on to say the Great Spirit include that the hearts of our forefathers to kindle the great council fire where the pipe of peace was smoked and the tomahawk buried. They took each other by the arms and called each other brothers. Black hearts became white towards one another. He has sent for them so that the council fire kindled by their forefathers may be rekindled by gathering the boards together because the fire was almost extinguished. He hoped when lighted the smoke would ever ascend in a straight column to the Great Spirit so that when the eyes of all of our people looked upon it they would remember the treaty of our forefathers.[7]

Chief Maskwaaki, probably the most powerful and influential Chief, got up and made a speech and he showed the great wampum belt of the Six Nations and explained it in a talk about it.

This wampum, according to the minutes, was three feet long and four inches wide. It had a row of white wampum in the centre running from one end to the other. The other, the representatives of wigwams, every now and then had a large wampum tie near the middle of the belt. It was given to the Nishnaabeg from the Nadaweg, at the time the French came to this country. The great council took place at Lake Superior. That the Nadaweg made the road and path and pointed out the various Council Fires that were to be kept lighted. The first marks on the wampum indicated the Council Fire should be kept burning at Bawating, this was referring to the meeting called by Shingwakoonse years ago. The second mark was the Council Fire at Manitoulin Island, where a beautiful whitefish was placed because of the Fish Clans, Atigimeg that predominated and were given the responsibility for keeping that fire. The third fire was placed in Georgian Bay and a beaver was asked to keep that fire. These were Ma'iingan's people and they were Amikwag. The fourth council fire was lit at Lake Simcoe, home of the Caribou Clan and the Maskwaaki people and they kept that fire. They were also given the responsibility of letting everyone else know when a meeting was going to be taking place. The Dish With One Spoon (there are different versions of how this came to be, this is ours) was an agreement between the Kanawake Mohawks and the Michi Saagiig Nishnaabeg in 1701, and they agreed they would share some territory. Maskwaaki understood that this meant the Six Nations could come and hunt while they were smoking the pipe with the Nishnaabeg. At the end of the American Revolution we gave them the land at Six Nations.

Maskwaaki is quoted as saying "the fifth mark represents the council fire that was placed at the River Credit where a beautiful white headed eagle was placed upon a very tall pine tree in order to watch the council fires and see if any ill winds blew on the smoke of the council fires. A dish was also placed at the Credit that the right of hunting on the north side of the lake was secured to the Nishnaabeg and that the Six Nations were not to hunt here, only when they came to smoke the Pipe of Peace with their Ojibway brethren."[8] This is very clear that Maskwaaki stated that the only time that this hunting could occur here is when the Nadaweg came to smoke the Pipe of Peace. The Six Nation people including the Mohawks at the Bay of Quinte at Tyendinaga were United Empire Loyalists, loyal to the British and were only given refuge by the Michi Saagiig Nishnaabeg. Their Chief Joseph Brandt reiterated openly that he thought he had more rights than that. However, it is clear by Maskwaaki's statement that he really had no right to Michi Saagiig Nishnaabeg territory. It was the Michi Saagiig Nishnaabeg who agreed with the crown to give some land to the Nadawag for their use, hence, the Haldimand tract grant was given to them and it is well documented that the Grand River Valley was given to them and we understand that it was squandered off and only now is the river considered First Nation. Anyone who claims sovereignty other than the bits of land they have from Michi Saagiig Nishnaabeg territory, they are wrong. No one has the right to hunt and fish in our territory, but us. The only time they can come and hunt or fish in our territory is to feed themselves when they come to smoke the Pipe of Peace with us. Any other interpretation is incorrect and I have heard that the Mohawks of the Bay of Quinte exert certain Aboriginal Rights other than the land that they were given. My advice to them is to tell them that they don't have Aboriginal Title to their land, the only title they may have is that they are refugees of the American Revolution and were harboured here on Michi Saagiig Nishnaabeg land by the British. Our hunting and fishing rights are protected by treaty, mainly the Crawford Treaty, the 1818 treaty and the 1819 east of here and any other treaty we have ever made we have declared that we have kept our hunting and fishing rights. This is very clear. It should be very clear to everyone especially to the Nadaweg and the Aayadowaad. When they claim sovereignty on Michi Saagiig Nishnaabeg land, they are very wrong. They are misrepresenting history.

Chi'Niibish/Deganawida

Deganawida is a very important being for the Nadaweg. We also have stories about him as well. My old people called him Chi'Niibish which means "big leaf." They say he was born at Zhooniyaagamig, Silver Lake also known as Lake Simcoe. The Nadaweg sometimes say Daganwida was Wendat and that he spoke with a stutter. My people believe he was Michi Saagiig Nishnaabeg and he learned Wendat. That is why he spoke differently—because he was not a native speaker. Our people lived at the narrows on Lake Simcoe hunting, and fishing. In the late 1500s, there were a mix of people living there—Wendat, Chippewa and Michi Saagiig Nishnaabeg especially around Kempenfelt Bay.

My old people say that Chi'NIibish was born on the shores of Zhooniyaagamig. They say he was a dreamer and that he had natural spiritual gifts. He had a dream that he would go all over and deliver a message of peace. In his life, he picked the Nadaweg to do this with.

Chi'Niibish started to get ready to do this by learning the Wendat language so he could communicate with the Nadaweg because their language was similar. He built a canoe for his journey, but not in the normal way. He built a spirit canoe, with the white part of the bark on the outside. He dreamed of how to do this. It was a very special canoe. It looked like a stone canoe. Nishnaabeg use these white canoes to travel spiritually. There are lots of references to these canoes at the Petrogylphs and in our stories. My old people said this canoe was an inverted birch bark canoe. This is a hard kind of canoe to make because the birch bark wants to curl the other way as it dries.

So Chi'Niibish dreamed for his journey and his work with the Nadaweg, learned the Wendat language and then built this spiritual canoe. He left the Lake Simcoe area in the late 1500s before Champlain got here and paddled across the lake to deliver his message of peace. He took the Michi Saagiig Nishnaabeg clan symbol of the bald eagle on top of a white pine tree. This was the eagle clan symbol. He worked with the Nadaweg for many years and they have their own stories about this. They buried their weapons in the roots of this great tree of peace.

Chi'Niibish said he would return to our territory, but he never did. The Michi Saagiig Nishnaabeg are messengers, spiritual people, diplomats, the people that go between. We live in the area between the Odawa and the Nadaweg. We consider him a special person with special powers. He had a strong Chibawbim and was a powerful dreamer. He had strong spiritual protectors and was very intelligent.

The Royal Proclamation and The Treaty of Niagara

I am related to the Georgian Bay people and the stories my family carries tell me that Pontiac was more of an Odawa person who lived around the south end of Lake Michigan. His colleague was Ma'iingan, who was from a long line of War Chiefs from the Amikwag—the Beaver people. Ma'iingan was much stronger than Pontiac in that he had more followers and more influence. Pontiac wanted Ma'iingan's help, but Ma'iingan said no. I don't know why. There is a break in the oral tradition and we don't know why. But if Ma'iingan had helped, things might have turned out differently because we may have been able to sustain Pontiac's war.

Our culture is such that we cannot sustain occupation. We have other responsibilities to our families and our communities and we always return home to take care of our loved ones, to hunt and fish. We do not have the machinery of war built into our culture, like the British.

The Royal Proclamation was a document made by the British. They had a meeting with the Nishnaabeg in 1762 because we were expressing worry over the 13 Colonies. They were expanding like crazy and had 1.5 million people living in them. The British took over from the French after the Treaty of Ghent. They called it the Seven Years War but they fought until bankruptcy. The 13 Colonies saved them in terms of resources—our resources were stolen to fight their war. The French only had about 20,000 people here at the time.

In 1760-62 the colonists found a route over the Appalachians. The Nishnaabeg went to the British, and said we're your allies. Protect our land. The British said yes and built a bunch of forts along the Appalachians. The British went back to Great Britain and wrote the Royal Proclamation. In hindsight, we know they were not going to try very hard to protect Indian land. In 1764, the British went to meet the 54 nations at Niagara which led to the Treaty of Niagara in 1765. The Treaty of Niagara and the 54 nation wampum would be a beautiful thing if the British had lived up to it and protected our land. The question is, did they give us sovereignty by saying they would protect our land or did they think it was theirs? In retrospect, we know they wanted our land and our resources. The Michi Saagiig Nishnaabeg were there and they were quite concerned with what was happening with the Shawnee, our neighbours to the south. Remember the Michi Saagiig Nishnaabeg had some villages they went to for part of the year on the north shore of Lake Erie. So they were neighbours with the Shawnee. The Seneca were not very nice to us and one of those creeks, I'm not sure which one, but near the mouth of the Grand River if you go due south, you hit a creek, go up the creek and as soon as you get to the bend you stop and walk up the mountain. Up over the mountain is where the Allegheny River is which connects you to the Mississippi. The Seneca went and took over that area. The Michi Saagiig Nishnaabeg who were friends with the Shawnee had to move the portage over to the west probably around Erie and it is a much longer portage and a steeper hill, but they did it.

The Michi Saagiig Nishnaabeg wanted to help the Shawnee protect the land from the Americans. That's where Tkamse (Tecumseh) comes in—he was fighting hard in 1771. The war of 1812 is just a continuation of the rebellion of the 13 colonies. He came up this way. There are not many cultural differences between the Chippewa'ag and the Michi Saagiig Nishnaabeg, we inter-married a lot. The Chippewa'ag and the Michi Saagiig Nishnaabeg were worried. I suspect that Tkamse came to Niagara. I know that the Chippewa'ag and the Michi Saagiig Nishnaabeg met him. He died fighting with the Chippewa'ag, October 5, 1813.

Because of these treaties that happened, there was a huge influx of settlers and the Michi Saagiig Nishnaabeg were displaced pretty quickly. They found themselves hungry and dispossessed of their usual places to get sustenance. They were starving. The women were complaining after the British took over. The women said that a lot of their activities—medicine picking, sugar bushing, and birch bark picking and all of those prime areas were being taking over by settlers. The Nishnaabeg did not understand this idea of private land that it would be owned exclusively by the settler. The Nishnaabeg thought they could still use that land. It didn't turn out that way. Later we know that the federal government transferred the responsibility for the land to the provinces. So through the process of making patented land, we lost a lot of our hunting grounds and food gathering grounds. When the treaty process happened and here they are, facing the British, the British came with some gifts, they were not as giving as the French. They came with booze, and that became a problem. The Nishnaabeg were losing ground here. Being marginalized. Not respected. Missionaries are trying to change our ways saying, don't follow your old ways, they aren't good. Speak English. Dress English. So many factors made it difficult for Nishnaabeg at the treaty site. They were begging for food. Buk-kwa-kwut says we need food. The women, Quenpinon said, the women don't want us to give up their areas. Quenpinon complains of being shot at. It was sign or starve. There is not a nation to nation respect here, like was thought of in the Royal Proclamation. This was not a sovereign to sovereign negotiation. This is not respect for our sovereignty. This is some other kind of process we are still grappling with. It was so unfair. And it became worse after the war of 1812. Like our 1818 treaty—basically they are saying we want to keep certain areas and things and the British just never wrote it in. They started promising money and then take it back. This is when Indian Agents were born and they would embezzle the money, then they would blame the Chiefs. Monies disappeared. Our land was encroached upon,

They had to move from the lake shore and north this way (Curve Lake). This whole package was annihilation—the proclamation, the 1818 treaty—exclusion, starvation, embezzlement of our monies, and forced relocation. Trying to hunt in areas where they were not allowed to hunt. Sneaking around. It was not a very nice time.

The War of 1812 and The Michi Saagiig Nishnaabeg

Much has been said about the War of 1812, and I don't want to rehash some of the descriptions of that conflict as written up by historians, I just want to make a few observations. I learned much of the story of the War of 1812 through the oral expression of my great uncle and his friends who talked about a relative, my great grandfather, five generations away by the name of George Taylor who was at Fort York and who fought there. It is said that George saw the Americans come in and they were taken by surprise one morning when the Americans showed up coming in big boats from across Lake Ontario. He said there were not that many British soldiers there and they did not fight very hard. They ran down the Indian Trail that is now highway 2 and disappeared and left it mostly to the Nishnaabeg to try and use guerilla tactics to give the Americans a hard time. Later, it is said that the British accused the Michi Saagiig Nishnaabeg of leaving the battle area and disappearing into the bush, but really all they were doing was organizing a sneak attack on the Americans and they were also waiting for other warriors to show up that had been giving the Americans a hard time across the lake. They paddled at night and subverted some of the American army's activities. William's story will be told in another chapter and there is an account of his life written up in the newspaper in 1910 and is included in the chapter about him.

Ashkiwinwininiwag

The interesting side to the War of 1812 is that the Michi Saagiig Nishnaabeg had a unit of fighters that they called the Ashkiwiwininiwag—guerilla style combative young men. They would paddle across the lake and give the Americans a hard time. They were particularly important in the battle of Niagara at Queenston Heights. When the Americans wanted to storm the river there was Michi Saagiig Nishnaabeg Ashkiwiwininiwag behind enemy lines getting rid of American recruits. My guess would be that in the American Army Annals they would say that their men were absconding because I read somewhere that young men did not want to cross the river because they heard war drums and that the Nadaweg was also helping the Michi Saagiig Nishnaabeg on that side of the river. William Taylor said there were at least 2,000 warriors there prepared to fight the Americans and the Americans got scared. That is the battle where Major-General Brock got killed. In Burlington Bay, there was a Michi Saagiig Nishnaabeg village that was feeding and housing the warriors that were fighting in Niagara and it was the Nishnaabegkwewag that were feeding them. According to the information that was given to the old men, there was upwards of 2,000-3,000 warriors at the height of activity.

One of the ways that the British accounted for the activities of the Nishnaabeg was to write them down. They had a beautiful account of some of the warriors, especially the Chiefs, that were active in the war. For the most part, they did not record any of the warriors. Hence the real numbers are not known. They were unrecorded. Hence they did not receive any pension as some people did and it was actually one of the contentious issues that came up later in the negotiations with the British that they neglected to record some of these names. The way the British dealt with this was to give out gifts to anyone for your participation in the war, but they didn't keep good records. Oral traditions say that the

Nishnaabeg took part in this war because they did not want the Americans to come. They had a bad reputation for mass killings and our relatives down below the lakes, especially the Shawnee (a lot of Nishnaabeg had married the Shawnee). It was a strong hatred and the Nishnaabeg decided to fight hard against them. The British on the other hand with all their soldiers, pomp and ceremony did not fight well according to my relatives. They did not have the courage and did not try that hard to stand up to the Americans.

George Taylor

There has been much said about the War of 1812. That war in which many Michi Saagiig Nishnaabeg fought. One of the individuals who fought in that war was one of my relatives, George Taylor. He was born on Buckhorn Lake around 1790. A story was written up about him in the *Daily Revue* on August 25th, 1900.

This is the article:

A REMARKABLE INDIAN
George Taylor Chemong Who Lived Until His Grandsons Became Grandfathers

A correspondent of the Christian Guardian writes: On June 18th at the Chemong reservation, there passed over to the great majority, in the person of George Taylor, an Ojibway Indian, one who, living to the extraordinary age of 110 years, was probably the oldest person in Canada. Born on a little island in Buckhorn Lake, a year before the province of Upper Canada was formed, this memorable centenarian spent nearly the whole of his days amidst nature's solitudes, trapping ahmeek (the beaver), or "in his birch canoe exalting," glided over the lakes and rivers enticing from the silent depths the Sugon (the bass), Maskenoza (the maskinonge). Only once during these long years did he forsake his peaceful pursuits and leave "the odours of the forest," and "the pleasant water courses," in response to a demand no patriot could resist. This was in 1812, on the invasion of this country by the forces of the American Republic. Then the call to arms re-echoed throughout the land, and George Taylor, a stalwart brave of 22 years, at once shouldered his musket, and like the never to be forgotten Tecumseh, joined the British forces for the defense of the rights of the sovereign and the protection of his native land. The loyalty of the brave redman, to the British Throne, however, was not something departed with the hot blood of youth. This was clearly demonstrated late autumn, on the outbreak of the present South African war. Visited one day by his pastor, in the course of a conversation, carried on amongst difficulties / he could speak little English and his visitor less Ojibway. He suddenly explained, "they tell me, sir, there is an awful war going on." Being told that such alas, was only too true, after a moments pause, a look of keen anxiety his bronzed and wrinkled face and in a voice tremulous with emotion he inquired, "do you think sir, the Queen's soldiers are going to be beaten?" On receiving assurances of a negative character, he breathed a sign of great relief and sat quietly back in his chair. Many years ago, this veteran first listened to this gospel story, from the lips of such men of God as John Sunday and Peter Jones, in his declining years, his life was brightened by a firm faith in a great spirit and the realities of the unseen world. To the last, he retained all of his faculties and was quite active. A remarkable fact in addition to his great age, was that he never suffered from the tooth ache, and possessed intact all the teeth provided by nature's hand. Very numerous are his descendants, for he had lived to see his grandsons become grandfathers.

The Michi Saagiig Nishnaabeg Clan System

There are a number of prominent people that have written about Clans—Eddie Benton Banai and Basil Johnson and other Nishnaabeg as well. There is also William Warren writing in the 1800s about his experience as an Nishnaabeg with mixed blood in the Minnesota area, and the American anthropologist Alfred Irving Hallowell. Even at this time, he writes that there were problems in understanding their clans the way he thought they should. Add another 150 years and there are more problems. However, during the last thirty or forty years, there has been a resurgence of people wanting to know their clans even though there is a lot of confusion, it is good for me to see that people are stepping back into Nishnaabewin and finding out who they are in terms of the clans.

The clan is like a last name in English, but it is hard to compare the two because there is so much meaning in the Clan system it can't really be compared. All the time I was growing up my clan was not clear. I was told different stories. One day in the 1970s, I decided that I would go and seek out my relatives in the Williams family. I asked my uncle Leland about it and he said he didn't really know and he wasn't sure. He told me to go and see Leland in Rama. He has since passed. I went to see Leland and I told him I was looking for the clan of the Williams family. He didn't answer me. He was very much a Christian man at that time and I felt he was trying to not deal with my question. About a year later, at a break in the middle of the meeting he came to me and said our clan is the Pike, specifically the Musky Pike, Maashginoozhe. We are the Fish Clan. We have a lot of relatives in through the Curve Lake area and through the waterway system between here and Georgian Bay. We are the descendants of the great Chief Maashginoozhe, who lived in around Lake Simcoe and Georgian Bay and also had relatives in this area because his sisters married in Michi Saagiig Nishnaabeg country. He identified himself both as Michi Saagiig Nishnaabeg and Chippewa'ag Nishnaabeg as they call themselves over there. Maashginoozhe, one of the leaders in the Georgian Bay area in the mid 1850s, who is also the son of Maashginoozhe, whose doodem was Maashginoozhe, met up with Paul Cane, the artist who travelled across North America to document and paint the list of First Nations Peoples and to document the terrain of North America. When he first left he travelled through the Toronto portage to Lake Simcoe, and he came upon a number of Nishnaabeg and one of them was Maashginoozhe, whom he painted. We have a painting of Maashginoozhe, my descendent. That has grounded me in terms of who I am.

I am not going to talk about each Clan because I think Basil Johnson has done that well and I admire his work. In the most recent times, people go and seek out their clans, and one of the problems is that they cannot decipher between chi-bawamin, your great dreaming, the one that you try and make contact with when you fast in the bush for four days. People confuse that journey in getting their chi-bawamin and their clan. They think whatever is coming to them, and messaging them in terms of spirit contact and making themselves available to them is their clan, when it is really chi-bawamin. You should not tell who your chi-bawamin is, but sometimes they do, thinking it is their clan. As an example, people will say to me, "I am from the Bear Clan", and I know there are no bears here in Curve Lake, unless they have moved in. I think it is their chi-bawamin, which they shouldn't tell people about, but speak to them in their quiet, private moments of prayer. People sometimes disagree with me if I correct them. We have Eagle Clan people here. We have Otter Clan people here, but some of them identify as Turtle. I ask one guy about that and he said he got it from a document and that his great great grandfather signed as a Turtle. That is confusing for me because I know that family is Eagle and I don't want to disagree with that great-great-grandfather. I am confused as why there are two clans mentioned.

Sometimes people asked Elders to find a clan for people. This process is not fool proof. I suggest that people try to find out through lineage and documents and talking to those old ones from their area rather than giving an Elder from somewhere else tobacco and asking for the clan. I am not sure Elders can retrieve a clan. I doubt that process, myself. Perhaps it can happen, rarely. I think what they are retrieving is the chi-bawamin.

The clans in this area at Curve Lake, when they signed the 1818 Treaty the clans were Eagle, Fish, Snake, a Black Duck in Lake Simcoe and the Reindeer or Caribou more so towards Chippewa'ag country around Cape Croker, Christian Island and Rama.

The Michi Saagiig Nishnaabeg are the people that traditionally lived on the North Shore of Lake Ontario and all of its rivers. The Michi Saagiig Nishnaabeg knew themselves as Nishnaabeg, first and foremost, and those Nishnaabeg were divided into clans and kin groups and families. It was very important for them to know their clan and to whom they were related to, because you could not marry within your clan. The women tended to be the ones to go off to other villages or other groups living in other areas to go and marry. Now that marriage, to another community also brought on other advantages. It allowed them to travel to other villages and be looked after by their clan in that village and that was important. Of course the women would have children, and those children would remember that their uncle, for example, was coming to visit and he would be from another group or community or another part of the territory. So it was very important to know your clan and that was a major reason to keep clans, so they could travel from one end of the territory to the other knowing that there are people that are friends to them, kin to them, and relations to them.

This part of Ontario was mainly occupied by the Crane Clan. There were others of course, but that was the main clan. The Crane Clan is the Chiefs Clan. The one I remember people talking about as being the main Ogimaa, or Head Chief was Potash, that came to this area along the Trent system and was on the east end of the north shore of Lake Ontario.

On the other end, which is at the bottom of the Toronto portage were the Eagles. The Eagles were very much a leadership clan with us, and maybe perhaps that's not recognized as such by the far end of the Lake Superior Nishnaabeg. When you listen to the Three Fires Midewiwin people speak, they say that the two leadership clans are the Loon and the Crane. We really didn't have the Loon Clan in this area. Our leading clans were the Eagle and the Crane.

Our Understanding of Treaties

The old people used to say they understood the treaties to be between the Nishnaabeg and the Zhaganash, between the two nations, two nations on equal footing. What has happened with the treaty making process in Canada is absurd—one-sided and absurd.

The Nishnaabeg always wanted to continue to live our lifestyle, our governance, our culture as we had always done. They thought that we had enough land to share some of it with the settlers. We were not giving up anything in making treaties.

The government approached these negotiations with a complete disregard for all of these. They promised things in round about ways—yes you can still hunt, fish and trap, just like everyone else. They forgot to add that we would be severly regulated to the point where we could not feed ourselves living off the land. The Nishnaabeg didn't understand the idea of private property. The government used this when it gave private property rights to the province. We were dispossessed of all of our lands other than the reserve. Trying to hunt and fish to sustain 100 families on five square miles of land was impossible. They knew it and we knew it. We starved when the provincial fishing season closed from October to March and deer season was only open for two weeks in November—the hardest time of the year to begin with. We were only allowed one deer per family. This is how much they restricted our food. Fur bearing animals were regulated by the province and the season only lasted from mid-October to April 15.

It has always baffled me that the written treaty records are so vastly different than our oral tradition. The government made all kinds of promises without writing them down. That's why the oral tradition is so important, although nobody believed us until very recently—the last 50 years, that's recent. Our people have been fighting for our way of life for hundreds of years.

Eniigaanzijig

The government has consistently used divide and conquer tactics against us. That's how the Medal Indians were born and they became the *Indian Act* Chiefs. The Medal Indians were called that because they were the ones that would break away from the collective in exchange for medals, gifts or army jackets. They were the sell-outs. There is a big difference between our old style leadership and Medal Indian leadership. The old man Jimkoons didn't like the word Ogimaa. He didn't understand it to mean Chief. He used it for those Medal Indians. He used the word Eniigaanzijig—a community leader, a clan leader, the one who can build consensus. It is from the word Niigaan—the one who walks ahead of everyone. The War Chiefs were Niigaan Niigaza—the one who fights ahead. Niigaanzinini would be head of a clan. That old style of leadership was very democratic because the community had to recognize you as a leader. The people had to recognize you as one that sacrificed for the good of the collective, as someone who could bring people together and build consensus. Sure the clan system was involved with the Eagle Clan and the Crane Clan being our leadership clans, and heredity helped, but ultimately one's authority came from their actions and the community's response to those actions. The Eniigaanzijig would have to build consensus between the Clans, the war chiefs, the civil leaders, the grandmother councils, and the women. The women were a powerful influence because they decided when and where the camp would be moved—and this was the foundation of our lives.

Our 1818 Treaty

The treaty of 1818 is remembered by story by my Elders and it's important I think to put down on paper what they remembered because the treaty of 1818 is the beginning of many deceitful activities by the government against the Michi Saagiig Nishnaabeg. The reason I say that is because the old people remember that they kept many of those things that would help them live on the land and sustain their way of life forever. They finally agreed after some negotiations that they would "sell" the land to whom the negotiators on the other side said the land was needed for farming.

Now, the Chiefs of that time who are listed on the treaty spoke pointing out certain things, that they were in a starving situation, they had lost a lot of their Elders and therefore they couldn't be guided as well as they should. They said that their women and children were having a hard time. One can see the duress our people were starting to encounter with settlement moving in around them, particularly in the Fort York and Fort Henry (Kingston) area.

The import thing here is that the older ones remember what they kept in terms of maintaining their sustenance. They wanted to keep the islands, all through the system because they knew they needed to have somewhere to pitch their wigwamin. They also requested that all of the river mouths on Lake Ontario be kept for them because this is the place they would catch the salmon they depended a lot on. They also wanted to keep the maple bushes of the women so that they could collect maple sap and make maple sugar. They also wanted to keep the rice beds, so they could pick rice. They wanted to keep wetlands for medicines and beaver houses, because they needed the beaver. Trapping was important at that time and the beaver were disappearing. They also thought that they could hunt along every shore, camp if need be on every shore in their territory and that the farmer would only stick to the fields and would have an understanding of their way of life. So the old ones, they believed in the government. They believed in their word. Some of the Chiefs and later in the treaties mentioned that the word of the government is good. But the government did not include any of those things in the treaty, except to save the islands. The islands were also vague in terms of which ones were saved. There was a later drowning of lands by dams, which eliminated islands and created islands, which later the government said they weren't original islands—so they were not included in the treaty. Thirty years later, the government made another treaty so they could sell the islands, arguing that they could not continue to pay for the Church and the maintenance of the school without government money. This is really unbelievable that we had to pay for our own colonization and demise.

There were many things starting to happen in the early 1800s that determined some of the results that were written into the 1818 treaty. For example, previous to this, perhaps 30 or 20 years prior the Gun Shot Treaty and the Toronto Purchase were made. These treaties were done on the run so to speak, by younger British Officers who lost documents and did not record well the negotiated settlements. Nevertheless, settlements started to occur legally after this in much of the shore from Kingston to Niagara was being targeted by squatters and this prompted much activity in the relationship between the governments and the First Nations people. As an example of what happened around the Gun Shot treaty and the Toronto Purchase, the government would soon find out that they did this wrong and went back to the Chiefs that signed the Gun Shot treaty and made them sign a blank piece of paper, saying that they had agreed to the Gun Shot treaty. They also renegotiated the Toronto purchase in 1805 after it had been made in 1787. This goes to show how confusing the situation was and signing of the treaty around the Toronto area the 13A treaty, the Chief or the spokesman at the time by the name of Quenepenon, which means "someone who ties in a reverse order." This spokesman or Chief said in 1805, that settlers were being hard on the Michi Saagiig Nishnaabeg in the Toronto area and were driving them away. Farmers would call their dogs on them and some of them were shooting at the Michi Saagiig Nishnaabeg. So there was a lot happening at that time in terms of creating the relationship that was the context for the 1818 treaty.

The 1818 treaty was signed on the lakeshore at what is now known as Cobourg. Cobourg sits at the bottom of the portage that went from the south west end of Rice Lake down to Lake Ontario. This is one of the reasons they would meet there, because this treaty was signing away "the back parts of the Newcastle district."

At this treaty there was a number of individuals that suddenly appear that did not take part in the negotiations around the Toronto area. Buk-kwa-kwut, the Chief or spokesperson for that treaty of the Eagle Clan came out of nowhere it seems and started to be the spokesperson. Paudash was also there who gave himself the credit of clearing the Trent River valley of Nadaweg and that he presented as a Grand Chief of sorts, but then he took second place at this treaty and the spokesperson was Buk-kwa-kwut (spelled Buckquaquot in Treaty 20, meaning "ball").

Buk-kwa-kwut made several points during the negotiations of this treaty. A lot of what he said was not included in the treaty. He did make several points that made it in—they were having problems with settlers, their former hunting grounds were being challenged by people settling on them, and he felt that if he did not sign this treaty his women and children would starve because his hunting area was taken. He also made mention that he was a young man, not being led by his Elders and he wanted to stress that. He also said that they were starving and they would like to have some food. The interpretation of these negotiations is also suspect. It would seem that the minutes as they are recorded do not include those things that are remembered in our oral traditions—to keep the rice beds, the river mouths, and the sugar bushes, was not recorded. It seems that this is the practice that has developed over time starting at this time.

Many stories are told around this time where the government did not fulfill any of their promises. The idea that we would continue to live on the land and use this as our sustenance obviously was not in the plan of the negotiators on the government's side. Coupled with all of this of course were the missionaries who were encroaching at the same time, trying to convince our people that living on the land was not the way to go and agriculture was promoted zealously by the Christians and they convinced my people that what they were doing was actually not conducive to their well-being. I believe that some of what was interpreted as Buk-kwa-kwut was twisted so it could accommodate government goals and missionary values. It was deceitful. It was the beginning of the end of respect for the way we live on the land.

Another factor that should be mentioned here is that this is one of the first treaties that guaranteed an annuity payment to our people. A sum of 12,000 pounds was paid then, plus we would receive 740 pounds annually. This was called by our people "newt-ee" money, which they were receiving up until 1960. However, what had happened though, the government came back around 1822 and said to the Michi Saagiig Nishnaabeg that they could not pay the 740 pounds forever, so they would only pay it to the ones that were alive in 1818 until they died. The payment would then be satisfied. The government used the interest from the 12,000 pounds to pay the "newt-ee." They held it in trust—they never actually gave it to us. They got the Indian Agent to take care of it for us. We know historically that this arrangement was a poor one because much of the monies supposedly held for us were embezzled.

The stories I heard from the Elders that I was raised by was that they remember this time around the early 1800s as being a very challenging time and they say that had to be really careful because they said "the whitemen" or zhaganashi would steal their furs by force, abuse the women, and would beat them up. When they complained to authorities, nothing was done about it. In fact, it became such a problem that the First Nations of Rice and Mud Lake petitioned Sir John Colborne. There was a writer in Curve Lake who was educated and could write very good letters—James McCue. He wrote several letters. This was a very difficult time. After the signing of the 1818 treaty, settlers moved into the area very quickly and displaced a lot of our people in their homeland, which they and their families had used for hundreds of years.

The settlers were hungry like sharks. Exploitation was common. Disease and starvation were widespread. Our people were being displaced from their camping areas, and we were "suddenly becoming a problem."

Coupled with all of this is the War of 1812. Where despite all the difficulties that were happening with our people, they fought on the side of the British and really helped the people on the north shore of Lake Ontario to fight off the Americans. The Michi Saagiig Nishnaabeg in particular practiced guerilla warfare below the lakes and this I believe turned the tide. The old ones I was raised by talked about the Michi Saagiig Nishnaabeg fighters who took no glory, took no money, took no medals, but got the job accomplished. There is no written record of them—only those ones that were living around Fort York and considered themselves as Chiefs. We call them the Christian Indians and they took a lot of credit for the defeat of the Americas. The true defenders were the ones that lived on the land because they could paddle down in there in the night and do damage.

Formation of Mud Lake Reserve

So the 1818 treaty was signed and renegotiated in 1822 where less money was promised and then it was decided by someone to try and start a reserve system in Ontario. The missionary society from Boston called the New England Company was asked to try and get the people of the north shore of Lake Ontario into living a village style of life and to Christianize them. This would be sanctioned by the government. The monies to do this was taken from the money that was held in trust by the government in signing the treaties. The New England Company started these First Nations communities in and around the time settlement was starting to occur in the Peterborough area, simultaneously the Peter Robinson immigration was occurring. Peter Robinson was a British army officer. The Irish settlement that happened here was a big influx and I sense that it was under pressure from Peter Robinson and the Canada Company and the like that the New England Company should centralize the Indians and not stand in the way of settlement. I think this is the way that Mud Lake or Curve Lake and Rice Lake were born. They also centralized the Michi Saagiig Nishnaabeg living around Kingston to Grape Island. It was a very difficult time. Many of our people were living around Rice Lake and Lake Ontario and slowly ended up showing up in Curve Lake because it was more of a distance from settlers and the settlement and they found some refuge here. The hunting was still good in this area. The north end of Chemong became the site for the reserve. However, I found out later it was a piece of land the settlers did not want, they felt it was too rocky and they thought it was best to "let the Indians have it." Actually it was only by their own misguided way that they inadvertently gave our people land which became really good hunting grounds. They didn't mean to do that. They just wanted the Michi Saagiig Nishnaabeg out of the way.

After the 1818 treaty of the Peterborough area from Rice Lake on north, surveyors moved in right away to survey the land. They sectioned it off very quickly and we know now in retrospect that they very much had settlement in mind. Seven years after the signing of that treaty a mass migration happened in this year lead by Peter Robinson. He brought Irish immigrants to the area and literally gave them free land. Yes, they paid 10 schillings for the first 100 acres and if they cleared that land, they got another 100 acres for free. Of course this is to the detriment of the Michi Saagiig Nishnaabeg who were being displaced very quickly. They were being shoved aside. It became clear that their expectation, that they would be let to live on the land as they always had along the shorelines and the farmers would farm the land away from the shorelines, evaporated into thin air. There were some reports that came from this area in around 1830s when the Strickland family moved in, known as Susanna Moodie and Catherine Parr Trail along with their brother Cornel Same Strickland, who saw themselves as friends to the local Michi Saagiig Nishnaabeg, but in the end they really didn't do anything about us being displaced from the land. We continued to live our lifestyle as much as possible, living along the shorelines and hunting in the swamps and bogs away from settlements. No one seemed to care at that time if we fished or picked wild rice. This kept starvation away from us, but not far. Any negotiations that happened between us and the government mentioned this difficulty. The government and the missionary societies of the day thought best to get people together into one area, one village, into one point of containment. Of course later this became known as the reserve system. That started in this area where the government gave some responsibilities to the missionary societies to gather all the Nishnaabeg and the three reserves popped up—Rice Lake village, later known as Hiawatha, the Grape Island community on Bay of Quinte, later moved to Alderville and the Mud Lake people later became known as the Curve Lake people. One of the Chiefs of the Curve Lake People by the name of John Crane moved on to Balsam Lake and then Scugog Island to try and get a life going there. There was much pressure on our people and the Chiefs to entertain the farming life and they were being courted by the missionaries to change their ways and to accept Christianity. Our people did accept some of this, in the light of much pressure to give up their old life and to also pacify the missionaries. Much energy was

spent by the missionaries to convert our people to Christianity and
there are many stories about this written up by the missionaries and
government agents who described some of the difficulties. There is
a classic report done by a government agent showing how stubborn
our people were. I was told of a man, a Nishnaabeg Michi Saagiig
man who did not like the idea of being contained in a small village so
he moved to an island in Gannon's Narrows and today that island is
named after him—Keshigo Island. He objected to our people being
Christianized and he came to be known as one who would laugh-
ingly moon people as they canoed by. He thought they were selling
out to the government.

In around the time of the start of the reserve at Curve Lake in
1829 the government also started to recognize Chiefs or Headman,
mainly Peter Nogie or Nogee. Nogee I think is short form for a
bowl or a plate and the Chief and Headman of the area but his
name cannot be traced to the names that are shown up in the 1818
treaty. Somewhere in there, probably at the time of the formation
of the reserve, the government changed these peoples names from
Nishnaabeg names to English names and they didn't document the
names. It is hard to trace the link. For sure, Peter Nogee and another
headman, Squire Martin would have signed the treaties in the area.

There was another headman by the name of John Crane. Crane
was a strong clan in the area. He came to the village at the height of
Chemung, now known as Curve Lake. He didn't like it and moved
to Balsam Lake and then to Scugog, where the reserve is today. An
interesting story is told about him. When he moved to Balsam Lake,
the government agent promised houses. The government agent hired
a white man to build the houses. The white man embezzled the
money and the houses were never built. Eventually, another man
built the houses, but they were not accepted by the community
and they eventually abandoned Balsam Lake and moved to Scugog.
James McCue, a member of Curve Lake who was schooled and could
write wrote letters about this.

The government reports of the day were telling of how much framing the Michi Saagiig Nishnaabeg had accepted and how Christianized they had become. Peter Nogee as an example was given some responsibility to handle some government money (that really belonged to our people but was managed by an Indian Agent). According to the Indian Agent, he embezzled it and was banished. He moved to live in around the north shore of Pigeon Lake and that place became known as Nogee's Creek. He lived there until he died. I think that what happened is that these monies that were owned by the First Nation because of the selling of the land in 1818 and in other treaties was being managed by Indian Agents who in turn did not have to account for a lot of the money. I think if money was lost it was easy on the part of Indian Agents, it was easy to blame the Chiefs for embezzlement. It occurred in other areas later on.

Our people did not embrace Christianity and being colonized with the fervor reported by the government. One example is Keshigo, and the island we named after him. He was very critical of the First Nations people for embracing this. Keshigo left the community and went and lived as an Nishnaabeg on this island without a lot of contact from the outside. That was his resistance.

The Williams Treaty

The 1923 Williams Treaty was devastating to my people. I witnessed the trauma and the fear that was put on my people that were trying to live on the land. They lived daily watching over their backs and trying to maintain their lifestyle as Michi Saagiig Nishnaabeg. The government with the implementation of the "basket clause" was a sneaky way to get rid of us as people who enjoyed this part of our great land. These old men I hung around with such as Madden and Jimkoons lived a life where they had to live by sneaking around and feeling like they were "poachers." They resorted to catching other animals and harvesting those things that the government did not feel were part of those things they need to "protect" from us. These things included small animals, such as the groundhog and the porcupine, the muskrat for meat and other things were also eaten because we were forbidden from hunting game like deer (which was our staple) and we were also prohibited from fishing from October 15 to July 1 every year under provincial statutes. This process was devastating to people that lived on the land. They faced starvation. But you know, I witnessed where they would circumvent some of these things brought on by government. Such as posting of permanent Game Wardens on our tri-lakes here—Buckhorn, Chemong and Pigeon. That way we were able to survive somehow but I see where it was an undignified way of living on the land, an adjustment that didn't need to be made. It was particularly difficult to obtain food in the winter time and since fishing was prohibited it became a time of great suffering. People had to run up an account at the Whetung General Store to tie them over until the muskrat season opened in

April. So it was November to April that was quite difficult. Some people still had to fish and would do it at odd hours and would have to sneak around and not be seen. This is a very difficult thing to do in the winter time. As you know, anyone standing on the ice can be seen for miles and this is what the Game Warden would look out for and go out and chase my people. There were many stories told of how my people escaped the Game Warden. There were many stories of our people being caught, and going to court in Peterborough to be given fines for fishing out of season. Imagine the indignity on our people when they came in front of the Canadian courts.

Shkin

This is a story about the time soon after the Williams Treaty was signed in 1923, when our people thought they had agreed to keep hunting and fishing rights. Because many people in Curve Lake lived off the land—hunting, fishing, and food gathering—it would be important that they retain the right to continue those activities.

Unexpectedly—and contrary to our understanding of the original agreement—game wardens began to monitor the area, and started charging people for poaching. Our people fished, hunted and gathered in order to feed ourselves, to survive. We had been doing this forever and we didn't know we weren't supposed to.

It suddenly became a game of cat-and-mouse between the game wardens and the people living on their own homelands.

Amongst those people came a hunter who was legendary at getting away from the game wardens. His name was Shkin, short for Shkiiniwenh meaning young man and he knew every trick to get away from the game wardens. He was such a skilled paddler that two men in a canoe couldn't catch him.

In winter, Shkin would cover himself with a white sheet on the ice so people wouldn't see him fishing. He was also an extraordinary ice skater and would skate circles around the game wardens chasing him. Shkin made fun of them and their clumsiness, taunting them: "You can't catch me."

Shkin used the old style of skates, in which the blades tied onto your boots. One day the game warden appeared with a modern pair of tube skates in order to catch Shkin at his game and out-skate him. Shkin was ice fishing when he spotted the officer and swiftly took off.

This time, however, the game warden was gaining on him like never before, and the chase was on.

Shkin realized those modern skates were catching up to him and so he raced over to the dangerous part of the ice where he saw a big crack about 20 feet wide. He skated like a son-of-a gun, as fast as he had ever skated … and he jumped.

Shkin made it across the open water and looked back at the game warden who had to stop, unable to make the leap. Shkin gave a big yell: "See I told you, you would never catch me. Have a good day." And with that, it can be said that a big crack ultimately saved Shkin's butt.

As humorous as the ending of this story is, it also serves as a stark reminder of how the government attempted to keep food from our peoples. It is also a story of gratitude and to remember our ancestors, our heroes, so dearly for having endured so much.

We never gave up our right to eat, in the same way we never gave up our right to access river mouths, our namesake: Mississauga. But that is another story.

Sam Fawn

The resilience of my people is admirable. One of the ways they kept up their spirit was with humour. Many stories are told of the clutzy Game Wardens that were posted on the lakes to watch out for us. There are also some sad stories. Old Sam Fawn, after many years of carving axe handles, saving up money and making other items like that, was able to afford a cedar strip canoe from Peterborough. He went fishing on Fox Island out of provincial season. He was seen by the Game Warden who chased him. Sam beat him and came across from Fox Island to the mainland at Curve Lake. He put his canoe up on shore, turned it over and walked home. Everyone did that back in those days. Everyone knew each other's canoes. The Game Warden was watching him from Fox Island, and he sneaked over and seized that canoe. The canoe has never been seen again. Poor Sam Fawn, worked hard his whole life, trying to live off the land. I remember him as being one of the most gentle human beings that lived in Curve Lake. The trauma created by the 1923 Williams Treaty will be longed lived. It lives in our hearts. It can never be repaid by the government no matter what they do. The damage has been done. Many people have lived through this trauma who have now passed on. I remember them dearly and I hope that somehow there are no Game Wardens in the Happy Hunting Grounds.

Nogie's Creek

Chief Nogie was banished to Nogie's Creek. The Indian Agent banished him to that place because he was allegedly caught abusing band funds when he was the Chief. The missionaries wanted him banished there because they thought he was a thief and a bad influence. It was no problem for him—it was beautiful over there. James McCue was a writer and there are letters written to the government in the archives.

Jacob Crane

He was the Chief in Mud Lake, but he was from Scugog. He wanted to be part of Curve Lake, so he came, but he didn't like it. He then got some land from the Indian Agent at Balsam Lake. He was a descendant of the Nika, the Gooses. The Indian Agent gave some money to a carpenter from Peterborough to build a house. The carpenter never showed up for four or five years. Finally, he came to build the house. But Jacob was frustrated and went back to Scugog.

Road Allowances

Sometimes I have heard the Métis called "Road Allowance People". The Ministry of Natural Resources (MNR) defines Road Allowance as "an allowance (normally 66 feet in width) for a road laid out by a Crown surveyor, including a road allowance shown on an original township survey and a road allowance included on a Crown plan of subdivision." These areas were also important for Michi Saagiig Nishnaabeg. The roads weren't built right up to the lake. So we used these areas to camp. Eventually, the things we left at the road allowances were vandalized because the settlers didn't like us using the land.

Beaver Lake/Amik Zaagii'gan

In the late 1940s the Government of Ontario divided the land around Beaver Lake up and sold them only to white people for $25–$30 per lot. Broke my heart. That was the Taylor branch of the families hunting area—Beaver, Gold, Catchacoma and Michi Saagiig Nishnaabeg Lakes. We got pushed north to Bottle and Sucker Lake. They took the trapline from James Taylor between 1952–1954 because they said he wasn't using it. They said he wasn't harvesting enough animals and selling enough furs. The Williams side of the family, the Maskonoje's area was up and down the Coldwater portage going to Georgian Bay.

1923 Treaty

I often asked the old guy Madden about what happened with the 1923 treaty. Madden did not go to school and we both spoke the

Curve Lake Nishnaabegmowin. He was my family. We trusted each other. I was very interested in his understanding of the treaty. Why did they sign it?

The way he understood it from his Dad, who was a signatory to the treaty, was that they were negotiating the trapping grounds north of Haliburton. There was nothing about negotiating or giving up our rights around here. Madden said his Dad never talked about that. He only believed they were giving up the trapping rights north of Haliburton. They did not believe they were giving up their rights anywhere else. That is why they continued to hunt and trap and fish as they had always done after the treaty was signed. It was not until the Game Wardens showed up and began harassing them that there was a problem. This was a big surprise to our people. They had no understanding they were giving up their treaty rights. They would have never given up their ability to feed themselves.

After the 1818 treaty was signed the settlers didn't want Nishnaabeg living on "their" lands. They were fine with Nishnaabeg hunting or trapping on their land, but they didn't want us living on it. That is why the reserve was set up. Back then, people knew all the non-Native farmers. They knew the ones that were mean and they knew the ones that were kind and let them hunt and trap on their lands. They also would let them park their canoes on the shore. There were no big face-to-face conflicts until the 1940s and 1950s. At that time, there was a shift. There were a lot of non-Natives moving in from urban areas like Toronto and Peterborough. The white people had better jobs and cars. There were better roads. People could live rurally and commute to the city. They could afford cottages. These urban white people didn't have relationships with us. Their understanding of the land was different. They had no understanding of our way of life. They wouldn't let us park our canoes, pick berries, hunt, trap, fish, and they would get very mad if we did. The conflicts were daily.

1923 *Treaty Commission*

The treaty commissioners interviewed some of the members of our community, Curve Lake, here at the community hall. This commission was mandated to investigate the claims of the Michi Saagiig Nishnaabegs that some of our lands had not been surrendered. The Michi Saagiig Nishnaabeg had been petitioning the government to settle these claims because settlement had started to occur illegally on those lands and some of the Michi Saagiig Nishnaabeg wanted compensation. John Taylor is the son of George Taylor, who I mention in another part of the book. John Taylor appeared in front of the commission. He was born 100 years before appearing at the commission so he was born around 1823. He had another brother James, and many of the current members of Curve Lake are descendants of James and John. I am going to tell you some of the stories I was told around this. I will present some of the commission records unedited, as done by the interpreters and recorded in government records. This will be in contrast to the stories I am about to tell you. This is how our old people remembered these interviews.

John Taylor came to the commission to tell them of his story. Apparently, he started to tell his story—where he was born, where he was raised and the areas he travelled to, and the areas he believed were his family's hunting grounds. He was told by the commissioners that they didn't want to hear his story, that they would ask him questions. This was not the way we treated our old people. This was not our protocol. He was disappointed that the commissioners didn't really understand how to talk to him. He needed an interpreter and this was done by the Chief at the time, Dan Whetung. John Taylor had to be helped to come to the commission. He was quite aged and had to be carried into the hall. I can imagine the story he would have told, from the early 1800s on. He also would have remembered the stories of his father, George Taylor, who was born on Buckhorn lake in 1790. None of that story was told, and none of it was recorded.

George Taylor had a wide reputation of being an extremely good Michi Saagiig Nishnaabeg man who knew how to live on the land and he would have transferred this knowledge to John Taylor. This is a big omission on the part of the commissioners to not hear the true story of the Michi Saagiig Nishnaabeg, simply because they didn't know how to interview this old man, stating that they were only there to find out where his hunting territory was. Much information was missed by the commission by their arrogance as lawyers in that they were in fact guilty of wanting only specific information. The following is the account of John Taylor's story as written by the commission:

Another person they talked to was the Chief Dan Whetung. All through his interview he stresses that it was critical for his people to maintain their hunting and fishing rights. He kept talking about how we lost a lot of land during the flooding from the construction of the Trent Severn Waterway in 1844 and 1908. He talked about how Curve Lake reserve was originally 1,800 acres, and we lost 600 acres to flooding. He told the commissioners that of the 1,200 remaining acres only about 400 acres were suitable for cultivating. He stressed that in the 1919 treaty, they did not surrender the game and their hunting rights. He told them that before the flooding the game was out on the shore in the marshes. After the flood, the game was pushed inland onto private property and the marshes were then very deep. This made life for the people very difficult. All the land around the reserve was leased and placarded up—there was no place to hunt or trap. There was no place to go.

The Treaty Commission's Treatment of the Elders and Chiefs

The treaty commissioners were arrogant white lawyers from the city. They had no understanding of our way of life, our way of governance, or our political traditions. This is very clear in their treatment of our Elder James Taylor. Here is this old man, a grand storyteller, our knowledge holder, the keeper of our history and our stories and they don't even let him speak! So disrespectful. If you read the minutes from the treaty commission they treat our Chiefs and our Elders very rudely. They are shockingly brash. Our people would have withdrawn in that circumstance and you can see this in the way they answered the lawyers questions—they are short, abrupt, curt answers ... I don't know or "maybe" or "yeah, sure." They are resisting participating because they were so disrespected.

The Chief of Curve Lake, Dan Whetung was not even allowed to bring his lawyer into the interview. The commissioners made his lawyer wait outside in the parking lot. The questions were a set up. The commissioners had no interest in understanding Michi Saagiig Nishnaabeg history. They were interested in taking the land and documenting evidence that it wasn't ours and that we didn't use it. The lawyers were trying to trap our people into saying that they could just trap around Curve Lake.

The Construction of the Trent Severn Waterway

The construction of the Trent Severn Waterway was a tremendously destructive force for Michi Saagiig Nishnaabeg. There were no negotiations with our people before construction started. We were flooded twice—once in 1844, mainly to accommodate settlement and lumbering and another time in 1908. A series of locks and dams were built all over our river system, blocking the fish and the flow of the water. We lost so many graves—I still find cultural evidence of these graves around here. We were lucky that Nishnaabeg bury their dead inland a bit or it would have been much worse. We lost so many sacred spots—fasting spots and camp sites. We lost so much land and so many island to the flooding. The mercury levels in the fish increased because of the flooding and the amount of bark in the waterway from logging.

There are special rocks on Sandy Point in Pigeon Lake. Grinding Rocks. I think the old people did grinding there—maybe they ground up corn. There is also an island on the west side of Wagosh Minis (Fox Island) that has many Graves. Old Mary Game Taylor (née Williams) would find handmade beads—made out of bone or clam shells or made out of items we traded. Remember our people traded at Montreal and also Fort Albany.

The Trent Severn Waterway was the end of the salmon that migrated to Stoney Lake from Lake Ontario. A few got locked in Stoney Lake and I remember them as a kid, but they too eventually died out. Eels were also really important to our people and the Trent Severn Waterway killed them as well.

The flooding really impacted the wild rice. Chemong Lake used to be all wild rice. It was so thick across the whole lake. We had a path up the middle of the lake to canoe, otherwise it was all rice. The rice came back a few years after the first flood, and it came back again after the second flood.

The Trent Severn really opened our homeland up to settlers though. They came in droves, built cottages, put their sewage in the lake increasing the nutrient levels. This was very hard on the rice. Then they also sprayed chemicals in the lake to kill the aquatic plants so they could have nice areas to swim. Farmers also put nutrients and chemicals on their fields and this would run off into the lake. By the 1960s the rice was really set back. Through the 1960s and 1970s the mnr issued licenses to cottagers to put pellets in the lake to kill the weeds. The Trent Canal put these same pellets through the entire system. In 1975 Eurasian Milfoil killed everything off and clogged up the entire system.

The nutrients caused big algae blooms. The muskrat population crashed. The big flocks of Passenger pigeons disappeared in the late 1800s. Makoons born in 1875 remembers them, but Madden, born in 1895 didn't. Makoons also remembered seeing eagles. Neither of them had any memory of caribou, but they both remembered elk.

At this time someone also introduced large-mouth bass into the system. We used to have small mouth bass, perch, lake herring, eels and musky and the fish in Chemung. The large-mouth bass really took hold though. Carp were introduced in the 1940s the same time as pickerel.

One time George Sunday and John Jacobs went up river on Mitchel Lake frogging and they saw a huge scary fish. They'd never seen this fish before. They rushed home without stopping at Bobcageon camp. It was a carp.

Madden and School, Traditional Nishnaabeg Education

Madden hated school. There was a truant officer in Curve Lake, but Madden was really good at hiding from him. His mother tried to get him to go to school, but she finally gave up. In Nishnaabewin, your independence as a kid was treasured. You were warned about potential consequences, but you were allowed to make your own choice. Things played out as they were supposed to play out. Madden didn't go to school. He was very close to his grandparents so he had a very traditional Nishnaabeg education. Every morning he would leave the house and hide in the bush with the other kids that hated school. They lived off the land, hiding all day long. Sometimes they only ate berries all day. Madden was only caught once by the Truant Officer and taken to school by the scruff of the neck. It was probably the only time he was ever there! He didn't like school, church or the doctors.

When Madden got old, I used to look after him. Sometimes I would know he was very sick, but he would pretend he was fine to avoid going to the doctors. I used to take him anyway. He would be yelling "gegoo! gegoo!" I'd tell him he had to go. When we got there, he'd use his broken English and say "Hey doc, I feel good! Look! I can move my arms!". Then he'd wave his arms above his head. He died when he was 95, and I am happy that he died peacefully in his sleep at the senior's centre and not at the hospital.

Beaver Lake

That area is now known as the Kawartha Highlands, but it is the traditional territory of my forebearers. It was our hunting area. In the 1900s, the headman was my Great Grandfather George Taylor, Musky George, he was called. He was Otter Clan. They came from Credit via Scugog and ended up in Curve Lake in the late 1700s. Much movement was happening at that time. People moved to Curve Lake to get away from the lakeshore because there were too many settlers. They came to the backwoods. George Taylor would go and hunt and trap in that area, along with his son. Then the government introduced the registered trapline system in the 1930s and 1940s. Canada thinks it is crown land.

Dow Taylor, the son of George, got the trapline. He had a trapping cabin at the far end of the Beaver Lake and Musky had it before him. After the war, the situation changed. The government decided to sell the lakeshore around Katchecoma, Beaver, Michi Saagiig Nishnaabeg lakes to settlers who wanted a summer camp. So they subdivided the land into lots. No local could by them. No Nishnaabeg could buy them.

The government was selling those lots cheap. One individual said he paid $2.50 for a lot on Beaver Lake. I was talking to a guy in Buckhorn who told me that his family bought a lot on the north side of Michi Saagiig Nishnaabeg Lake for $30. He remembers that his dad had to pay more to survey the land, $60 then he paid for the land! Those lots are worth $300,000 today. That's our land.

At the same time, the government was taking land from us and selling it to white people, they took Dow's trapline because they said he wasn't using it. Some white person said that the beavers were running rampant and that Dow wasn't keeping it up. It was just that settler mentality! Urban people arrive in our area and they see beavers doing what they've always done and they complain that the beavers are taking over. They don't even share the land with beavers. In the Nishnaabeg philosophy you go up and take enough to pay your expenses. You take as many animals to support yourself and your family on the land. You don't take 200 beavers. Dow's trapline was given to a white person.

To make things worse, many years later they turned our land into a park. I think the government did that so it would pit allies— people who love parks against us. They saw where we could rightfully .claim the area and they put a stop to it because we could.

Our children will rightfully fight for that area.

We were never given any land on a treaty basis. None. We were a landless people until the missionaries "gave" us the land at Curve Lake—land they took from us to build a mission.

I still visit that old campsite on Beaver Lake where the trapping cabin was and I put tobacco.

Bullfrogs

Bullfrogs were always harvested by our people in June, for centuries. They were never a major food source for us, we preferred to eat fish, but nonetheless they were important to us. Sometimes we would sell them to lodges for extra cash. Sometimes we traded them, and we always ate them. I learned how to catch bullfrogs for food from Madden and Jimkoons.

There are two ways to catch bullfrogs. One way is to put bait onto a string and they will attack the bait. This is the way to do it during the day. At night, during the mating season in June, they move out into the bays for mating, and you can pick them up when they are moving. During June, the male's front paw swells and the thumb swells so it can grab the female when she is full of eggs. At night the males go far from the shore into the open water and sing. The females come out and find the best singer.

These sounds have now disappeared in the Kawarthas. Buckhorn and Chemong Lakes were the first to lose them. We've frogged in those lakes for centuries and there was always a population that went very deep in the bays that we couldn't catch. This maintained the population. It was all the changes to the lakes through the Trent Severn, the pollution and the virus that killed the bullfrogs, not Michi Saagiig Nishnaabeg harvesting them.

On June 11, 1977 I was with my son Keesic, who was just seven years old, and Wayne Bear (Taylor). We were on Crowe Lake on the Hastings county side, during the day bull frogging—just doing what we had always done as Michi Saagiig Nishnaabeg. We launched our canoe with Keesic in the middle and a lodge owner called the mnr and reported that Indians were fishing. We paddled across the lake into Peterborough County and were busy catching frogs, when the Game Wardens snuck up on our blind side and surprised us. They came out of nowhere. Wayne said "What the hell are you doing here?!" Of course this statement made it into court. I think he was genuinely surprised. We were all surprised.

I was in the front of the canoe and Wayne was paddling in the back. The Game Wardens were paddling a square stern canoe—the kind that you can put a motor on. I had always said that if I ever got caught fishing, I would take it to court. I believed that was important for recording purposes. The courts record everything in the court transcripts and I wanted a record of my defense—the oral tradition, our stories, our perspective. Otherwise, my grandchildren wouldn't even have that.

I asked the Game Wardens who they were, and I asked to see their badges. They told us that it was illegal to kill bull frogs because a law had been passed in Ontario the year before. I argued that that law doesn't impact us. They said it did. I told them we had treaty rights.

The Game Wardens took six frogs for evidence, and let 56 go. We had 62 in total. I asked them to let them go along the shore, every 20 feet, like we'd caught them, but they refused. They just dumped them all in the same spot, and wrote us a ticket to appear in court.

I hired a lawyer and went to trial. I could have won on a technicality, because remember the lodge owner who called the mnr was the one who witnessed us catching the frogs, and he was located in Hastings County, but the mnr charged us in Peterborough County. There was no witness in Peterborough County. I didn't want to win in a lower court. I wanted to fight on the basis of our treaty rights.

I was the Chief of Curve Lake at that time, so I had access to the minutes of the 1818 Treaty and the minutes from the 1923 Treaty Commission on the Williams Treaty. I wanted to challenge the 1923 Treaty because it is absurd. How can a civilized government and court system make a treaty that exterminates everything, absolutely everything for a people? I knew I would get convicted in the courts, but I wanted it on the record, for my children and for my grand-children. I wanted all the evidence there for them to see that Michi Saagiig Nishnaabeg people had been blatantly lied to in the treaty.

The trial was interesting. The Crown used a lot of tricks to try and discredit us. They brought in an amphibian scientist from the Royal Ontario Museum to talk about why the population of frogs was declining and the scientists pointed to the "Indian's fishing." We now know it was a virus.

We had support in the community from people and from coun-cilors. But in order to get it into the higher courts, we had to lose at provincial and district court. We got negative press, and it looks like the courts weren't believing me. Some of the councilors were making snarky remarks because the band was paying for my defense.

My defense was based upon the oral tradition and our under-standing of the treaties. This is said to be the first time in Canada that the oral tradition was used as evidence in a court case. The min-utes from the 1818 treaty clearly showed that our Chiefs understood that we had retained hunting and fishing rights in that treaty and Dan Whetung's testimony in the 1923 Williams Treaty Commission also demonstrated his understanding of retaining those rights. This is the story of our treaties from our old people—that we kept our hunting and fishing rights. That's the story. The courts had to accept it. The community was happy when we won the case.

For a long time, I thought that we had won something. Then the Howard Case negated our win in 1994. For a long time, I thought our rights would disappear. Now I am kind of excited again that Ontario is now recognizing the 1818 Treaty and we now have our hunting and fishing rights back. This is the first time in my life I have had those rights except for that brief period when the NDP Government under Premier Bob Rae gave us them back in that interim agreement. The Progressive Conservative Government under Mike Harris cancelled the agreement and our rights. But now we have them back. Maybe

Canada is capable of listening. Maybe Canada can look at us on an even footing. I'm not naïve, the treaty making process is a one sided process. There is no resolution. We are a sovereign people. That's the bottom line.

I want my grandchildren to have a space and a place to speak our language and live our traditions. I hope that the younger generations can appreciate the resistance of the older generations. Our people fought hard and for a very long time to continue our way of life. We didn't even know we were resisting and that's what happens with a good culture, one that has taken years and years and years to form. These cultures have an innate ability to protect themselves, to survive and to sustain.

Every Speck of Dust Has Been Raised By Our Feet

This is our land. This is our homeland. Everything here speaks to us about our old people. We've been here a long, long time. We were created here. This place is very much part of our soul, very much a part of our spirit. We were created here. There is archaeological evidence that we were here in Ontario 10,000 years ago. Specifically, I was speaking to an archaeologist that was looking at a site that was 9,500 years old. To him, these are archaic peoples who hunted caribou. But we tell our old stories about these peoples. Those people are our ancestors. We know that we have been here a long time. Every speck of dust in this part of Ontario has been raised by our feet. We have been all over. No matter where you go. When you talk about burial sites that is very specific. We don't talk about the land in that way. Every geological formation like rocks, every lake that we have, the Great Lakes, Niagara Falls—these all have particular meanings for us. It is in our blood. It is in our genes.

Development proceeds as a priority over us and our history. That is breaking a lot of sacred and natural laws. What I see around this is a big charade of development, and greed and money mongering without any respect for these sacred places. It bothers me that our people have to be moved a lot, from one spot to another. Those bodies are coming home to our reserves and being buried there. That is not the best thing to happen. The best thing to happen is that they be left alone, and those sacred places where they are buried could be left alone. I understand the argument that says development has to happen but why does development have to happen at our expense? What are people doing thinking they have every right to do this?

Who gave them that authority? Certainly when settlement was moving in here and treaty was being made, that is not something we gave up. Today we are told that we have no rights to our ancestors. Come on. That is your thinking, your way, your courts talking, your leaders talking, your wise men talking, your politicians talking and they are basically wrong. And they want to change the world, they want to change the earth, they want to change the shape of things, they want to move mountains and dam rivers. In the long run, there is a word in Nishnaabewin that is Aanjigone, which is like a karma. If you don't honour those natural laws and being, you'll pay in the future and I can see where the people that are from the western society are going to suffer in the future, because this type of living is not sustainable. We are going to pay for that in the future. I worry about my children. I worry about my children lots.

It seems to me all that is happening here is that some developer has come across a burial and we activate a process of having to look at this archaeologically. People scurry over there, and the Nishnaabeg get called. Pray over this, bring your colours, bring your tobacco, bring your cedar. The bones get reburied and nobody really cares. The development occurs. I don't get any money of this. The developers keep on building their high-rises and highways and roads and wells and everything else making lots of money on our land. That is what I mean, but what gives them this authority to violate our gravesites in this manner?

Who Depleted Our Fish Anyway?[29]

"Fishing season" conjures up many questions for me. We never had "seasons" for fishing. Who imposed them on us anyway? This idea of a "season" is imposed on Nishnaabeg by the governments of Ontario and Canada.

It seems to me this concept of a fishing season started after the signing of the 1923 Treaty. Our people thought they kept the right to fish, our traditional way of fishing without "government seasons," during the "negotiations". Soon after 1923, however, our people got a reality check: Curve Lakers started to be charged for "fishing out of season" and game wardens came and told us to not fish during the "off season." We had (and have) our own ways to use the fish without depleting them. The governments' restrictions became particularly hard as it meant food (i.e. fish) was kept from us. It became even more difficult in winter where food was lacking anyway.

This restriction on fishing in the winter soon worried our leadership and many Nishnaabeg in our area were concerned. So in 1932, a petition was sent to the governments by area Michi Saagiig Nishnaabeg to stress that we did not cede our traditional right to live on the land and waters; our people told the governments and their game wardens to back off. Over time, this petition didn't stop game wardens from enforcing the provincial seasonal fishing restrictions. To this day, we are still harassed when we practice traditional activities to acquire food.

The only good I see coming out of the 1932 position is that we let governments know that the 1923 Treaty is not a document that respects our traditional relationship to fishing. It would seem to me that this written word of theirs is wrong and therefore fraudulent. We are still, however, forbidden to fish free of provincial restrictions and the saga continues.

Despite the government's use of game wardens and the courts to harass us, we continue to practice living as Michi Saagiig Nishnaabeg on the land. We still hold gatherings, and we still go hunting and fishing. I admire this resistance as it shows a deep rooted desire to protect our identity as a distinct people who know that this territory was gifted to us by the Gzhwe Manidoo.

The settlers who moved into our lands are to blame for those regulations that harm us; it is them that the 1923 Treaty accommodates, so they can live off our lands. They are not exempt from abusing the fish on our homeland. We have paid heavily and our ways, such as our language, are threatened. We have been called "poachers," and "fishing machines who deplete fish stocks on area lakes."

However, what is missing from many settler narratives is the fact that they are the ones to blame for the decline of fish populations. I came across the following piece of writing from a book written by E. Guillet called Early Life of Upper Canada. In it, he writes about fishing by the settlers and describes the over-fishing practiced by the "pioneers." Guillet quotes an 1869 Federal Department of Fisheries report as saying:

> In early times [Wilmot's Creek, flowing through Clarke Township into Lake Ontario] was famous for salmon, great numbers of which frequented it every autumn for the purpose of spawning. They were so plentiful forty years ago that men killed them with clubs and pitchforks, women seined them with flannel petticoats, and settlers bought and paid for farms and built houses from the sale of salmon. Later they were taken by nets and spears, over a thousand often being caught in the course of one night[10].

In the period just previous to the War of 1812, hauls of whitefish of 1,000 or more were commonly taken at Niagara, and at almost any village on the shores of the Great Lakes. In later years, when fishing developed on a large scale, the hauls were much greater. A resident of Barrie recalled that he "once helped haul in a net near Willard's Beach, in Prince Edward County, that contained 14,000 fish." In some parts of Lakes Erie and Ontario single hauls of 90,000 white-fish were not unusual. In the Detroit River fish used to be driven into pens where they were captured and dried by the hundreds of thousands, to be used later as fertilizer; similarly, Lake Ontario whitefish were sold to farmers in the eighteen-sixties and used for manuring the land.[11]

As you can see, the settlers did much to get rid of fish from our territory. The salmon became extinct from our lakes. Whitefish were decimated.

Amazingly, we get blamed for the disappearance of our fish. We are in double jeopardy: our traditional food is gone and we get blamed for it. Ow-wee!

The Right Size for a Garden[12]

What size does a garden have to be before we call it a garden? Is planting one seed into a small mound of earth worthy of the name garden? And is gardening, if it's the act of planting seed, human's first manipulation of food? Or is it more primal than that?

Our Elders, the Nishnaabeg from the mist of time, would say that a garden is more primal than humans themselves. They would point out that the first garden occurred at the time of creation and the earth itself, call the Great Mother, is our garden put on this Earth Plain for us to use. This dawned on the Nishnaabeg early in time and they have painstakingly retained this knowledge.

That nature is our garden is so embedded in Nishnabeg worldview, one could say it's genetic! At the time of creation, human beings were told that everything they need to live, survive and prosper on this earth was ready and waiting. Everything found on Mother Earth then is an Nishnaabeg's garden, including fish, animals, plants, water and trees. These they harvested with care and ritual, obeying the Original Instructions given to them at the time of creation. One of these rituals is that one must drop tobacco before reaping any plant or animal.

Original Instructions are primal, not primitive, as the latter implies progress. Nishnaabeg believe that progress is by natural law a violation which will ultimately end in the destruction of humanity. One could say then that modern gardening is progressive and therefore, part of a lifestyle which will eventually show itself as destruction in the long run. Certainly, I see modern mega-agriculture already showing signs of destruction (especially when one considers the negative effects of pesticides, herbicides and insecticides).

A profound yet simple idea was innate in Nishnaabeg: whole-
some natural food will keep you alive until you die of old age. Food
is sustenance but one must view food as a healer to see it as it was
meant to be by the Gzhwe Manidoo.

When one sees food as a healer, one learns to combine or completely eat plants and animals without leaving a scrap: the strawberry
packs more healing punch if the green cap is eaten with the fruit (the
berry eaten in this way is credited by the Nishnaabeg for healing
them from the so-called Blanket Diseases[13]).

Another example is how westerners eat only filets of fish.
Everything on a fish is to be eaten except the bones and even they can
be used for other things. The true Nishnaabeg connoisseur is horrified by the wastage in fileting pickerel in the modern method: the
western diner is equally horrified by the way an Nishnaabeg eats fish.

For this reason, Nishnaabeg rarely eat traditionally in front of a
white man. This spring a white acquaintance walked in on me while
I was feasting on Muskie head and innards (the best parts). With the
usual Western naïve inquisitiveness, this person filled the air with
questions and curiosity. She gagged when I ate the eyes.

Some foods are more healing than others and fish fit that cat-
egory. The Elders say to ease up on red meat when you become a
grandfather (about age 50) and completely go off it when you become
a great-grandfather (about age 70). The main reason is that red meat
is difficult to digest and becomes sludge in your system. It causes
constipation and inflammation—two major factors in early aging.
Fish are to be eaten instead of red meats and a diet of whole fish will
tone the old body as if new.

The staple foods of the Nishnaabeg were fish, wild rice and fruit.
Wild rice can be stored and fruit dried, for use in winter, and fish can
be harvested as needed. The Nishnaabeg knew to eat more plants
than meats and some cultivation occurred. They would plant beans
and corn in open areas in the springtime and harvest them in the
autumn. These plants required planting but needed little care when
planted together. They were also dried to be used during the winter.

The Three Sisters, as corn, beans, and squash were called by our sisters and brothers to the south, apparently will give you a complete diet containing protein, carbohydrates and roughage. When combined with fish you have more than a complete diet—in moderation, of course, and without the introduction of artificial oils.

At times, food from nature's garden is readily prepared for you while at other times it is rather difficult to harvest these foods. Berries are easy to harvest in season, but it takes patience to pick them in bulk, and it is an art to dry and store them properly. Wild animals are not easy to catch and harvest and it seems to me the Gzhwe Manidoo designed life that way. One must be physically fit and mentally alert to survive, and balance appears to be the key. If one has food, ready and prepared, available at all times, then there would be a tendency to deprive oneself of exercise and hence, one is out of balance.

In the modern context, the problem we seem to have is a critical drifting away from natural laws and the Original Instructions. Our Nishnaabeg forefathers knew a long time ago what western medicine is now just beginning to find out. Exercise and eat a balanced diet containing only small amounts of red meat only. Many of the Nishnaabeg themselves have also been caught up in this vicious modern cycle of eating as a consumer at the bottom of a pyramid of mass food production. Their modern diseases are an indication that this is so. Some Nishnaabeg Elders still practice the Original Instruction, either in whole or in part, but it is getting increasingly difficult for them to do so. Everyone is under pressure, and we seem to know there is something wrong but we can't put our finger on it. Is it simply runaway greed for the almighty dollar where we completely lose any of our sacred beginnings?

It was said by our Nishnaabeg forefathers that there will come a day when life will hang by a spider web—that human beings will come close to total and complete death if the Original Instructions are not followed.

"How do we know we have reached this stage?" I asked an Elder. He said, "When the trees begin to die from the top, and it will take some years, and when this death on the trees reaches to the height of man, humans will die."

There is a cure and it is as simple as being in the human's hand. The prophecies say that children soon to be born may have to save us if we don't do it ourselves. Our Elders see a brighter day but unfortunately, that day seems to be eluding us all.

Wiigwamin[14]

The Elder and I were laughing at the silly questions I was asking him about shelter. I was quizzing him about the old days and how people had slept in a domed-shaped wigwam. I had assumed that our ancestors lay alongside the fire that burned in the centre of the lodge. The Elder smiled and was quick to point out that they slept fanned out from the centre, with their feet next to the fire and their heads furthest from the flame. As my questions got sillier, and the Elder more amused, I realized that I was assuming the bias of a western and "civilized" point of view.

The wigwam was built with poles or saplings. Birchbark and bulrushes were tied together with green basswood bark and basswood twine. The poles were planted in the ground, brought together in arches and covered with mats. These poles were left at the camp site and the coverings were carried from place to place.

"Why didn't you invent lumber, nails, cement and bricks?" I teased. He repeated my question to make sure he had heard it right and then with gentle seriousness said, "Because they were not included by the Gzhwe Manidoo in the Original Instructions".

"But lumber is trees, nails are mined from the Earth and the bricks and cement come from rocks and sand. What difference does it make?" I asked.

"It's a matter of life and death."

The Original Instructions separate the life path into two parts: that which promotes life and that which ends in destruction.

I continued to press the Elder. "Surely building with nails, bricks and cements is easier than using sapling and basswood bark. This is progress and technological advancement!"

"What do you mean?" he asked.

"I mean that progress is better and therefore easier." I explained.

"There is no such thing as progress, only change," he reminded me. "I think you're asking me to explain how and why people do things the way they do today. You've lost me. You're asking me to describe a moose when you only allow me to feel the hoof!"

"Let's talk about wiigwamin (shelter)," I said boldly.

"It seems to me that this is what we're talking about." He explained. "When we discuss wiigwamin, we are talking about life itself. We can't separate it into little parts; everything on Earth is connected. We must ask constantly whether anything, like this progress you mention fits into the Original Instructions. The question in the modern context should be whether the direction we are embarking on is for, or against nature. If we kill even the smallest creature and threaten it with extinction, then we are not obeying the laws of our Gzhwe Manidoo, as they were given originally."

The Elder was forcing me to ask fundamental questions about technology. I wondered how often during my brief time on Earth I have witnessed changes about which I should have been skeptical. The feeling of having been blindly led overwhelmed me.

I thought of the manmade changes since the 1940s; a mere fifty years. In the 1940s there was no hydro in the village where I live; there was no tv and no plumbing. There were none of the modern conveniences that we take for granted today. There were no commercial jets, no computers, no microwave ovens, no Xerox machines, no tape recorders, no stereo music. There were no vcrs, no air conditioning, no washing machines, dryers and no touch dialing. There were no freeways, shopping centres, or malls. No K-mart and no Wal-Mart.

The Elder had watched these changes too. He lived a modest lifestyle. We wore used clothing. I realized that he didn't create garbage. He was a natural recycler, a true human being living in modern times.

To get back to the topic I asked, "What did our ancestors do to keep warm in their wigwams in 30 to 40 below zero temperatures?"

"The seniors of each family kept the fire going all night, " he replied. "Their role was to gather dry wood ahead of time and keep the whole family warm."

"The seniors felt needed?" I asked.

"Yes, unlike today when we put them in homes by themselves." His voice drifted off.

There was a long silence as I watched him eat. I asked him about the little dish in which he had placed some food. He told me that many Nishnaabeg traditionally made offerings of part of their meal. "At the end of the evening, I add food to a bowl of table scraps and put them outside for the birds and animals," he said.

I watched him as he went out into the night and climbed a small grassy hill behind the house, put the dish down and then stood for a few moments. When he came back into the house he said, "In five minutes the bowl will be empty."

The Elder was free of commodified culture. Corporations like Wal-Mart would not like him. Living in Canada today, there is scarcely a moment when you are not in contact with a corporation. Indirectly, at least, most people work for corporations. Their daily schedule is determined by corporate needs. They dress and behave according to corporate concepts, they interact with machines, and they spend their days living inside corporate rhythms. The building they live in was probably created by a corporation, as was the furniture, appliances, antiperspirants—all the result of corporate ideas and dictum.

The Elder lived in a "house" but I had the feeling he did so because the forces which made him do it were overwhelming. I felt that if the times changed for the better, he would adapt more readily than most. He told me that he set up a wigwam frame, covered with canvas, every summer.

"I sleep in the wigwam every night so I can hear the wind and the rain. I can really feel the Great Spirit then," he said.

I found myself deep in thought, staring at the Elder. I was looking at a man who challenges all things "Canadian." He knew where he stood in the bigger picture and it intrigued me that he was confident and full of hope, despite the obvious gloom of modern society. This great man was materially poor. He would be called "lazy" by many but I understand why he chose to disassociate himself from the workforce. He knew that to become a pawn in the corporate rhythm would be dehumanizing and lead him down the path to ultimate destruction.

The Elder never wished to be part of this so-called "civilized" society, this machine, and he is not. He lives on the fringes of the technical world, but is still aware of certain fundamental truths. The most important require a reverence for the Earth—a reverence that is subversive to Western society and its technology.

The Elder must have wondered why I was staring at him but he did not say anything. It was time to go. I thanked him with a gift of tobacco and walked home. While lumbering to my place, I pondered his words and wondered why I had received Truth instead of an interview full of specific information on Nishnaabeg shelter.

At home I had been reading back issues of *Akesasne Notes*, a native newspaper, and the following text from 1977 struck me. In that year, forty-one years ago, the Iroquois made the following presentation to the UN Conference on Indigenous Peoples. How coincidental, I thought.

> *In the beginning we were told that the human beings who walk about on the Earth have been provided with all the things necessary for life. We were instructed to carry a love for one another, and to show a great respect for all beings of this Earth.*
>
> *We were shown that our life exists with the tree life, that our well-being depends on the well-being of the Vegetable Life, that we are close relatives of the four-legged beings.*
>
> *The Original Instructions direct that we who walk about on Earth are to express a great respect, an affection and a gratitude towards all the spirits which create and support Life. When people*

cease to respect and express gratitude for these many things, then all life will be destroyed, and human life on this planet will come to an end. To this day the territories we still hold are filled with trees, animals, and the other gifts from the Creation. In these places we will receive our nourishment from our Mother Earth.

The Indo-European people who have colonized our lands have shown very little respect for the things that create and support Life. We believe that these people ceased their respect for the world a long time ago. Many thousands of years ago, all the people of the world believed in the same Way of Life, that of harmony with the Universe. All lived according to the Natural Ways.

Today the species of Man is facing a question of its very survival. The way of life known as Western Civilization is on a death path on which our own culture has no viable answers. When faced with the reality of their own destructiveness, they can only go forward into areas of more efficient destruction.

The air is foul, the waters poisoned, the trees dying, the animals are disappearing. We think even the systems of weather are changing. Our ancient teachings warned us that if Man interfered with the Natural Laws, these things would come to be. When the last of the Natural Way of Life is gone, all hope for human survival will be gone with it. And our Way of Life is fast disappearing, a victim of the destructive processes.

The technologies and social systems which destroyed the animal and the plant life are destroying the Native People. We know there are many people in the world who can quickly grasp the intent of our message. But our experience has taught us that there are a few who are willing to seek out a method for moving toward any real change.

The majority of the world does not find its roots in Western culture or tradition. The Majority of the world finds its roots in the Natural World, and it is the Natural World, and the traditions of the Natural World, which must prevail.

We must all consciously and continuously challenge every model, every program, and every process that the West tries to force upon us. The people who are living on this planet need to break with the narrow concept of human liberation, and begin to see liberation as something that needs to be extended to the whole of the Natural World. What is needed is the liberation of all things that support Life—the air, the water, the trees—all the things which support the sacred web of Life.

The Native Peoples of the Western Hemisphere can contribute to the survival potential of the human species. The majority of our people still live in accordance with the traditions which find their roots is the Mother Earth. But the Native People have need of a forum in which our voice can be heard. And, we need alliances with other people of the world to assist in our struggle to regain and maintain our ancestral lands and to protect the Way of Life we follow.

The traditional Native People hold the key to the reveal of the processes in Western Civilization, which hold the promise of unimaginable future suffering and destruction, Spiritualism is the highest form of political consciousness. And we, the Native People of the Western Hemisphere, are among the world's surviving proprietors of that kind of consciousness. Our cultures are among the most ancient continuously existing cultures of the world. We are the spiritual guardians of this place. We are here to impart the message.[15]

Water Circle[16]

At dusk in Curve Lake, Ontario, sitting in Alice and Doug Williams's living room beside Buckhorn Lake, Alice (Minwaajmod-kwe) and Doug (Gitiga-Migizi), Wilma Jacobs-Taylor (Miigwewin-kwe) and Winston Taylor (Minwaajmod) reflected on the importance of water for the Nishnaabeg people.

DOUG: I think that we should talk in a circle, beginning with you, Julie. Why water? Tell us why you are doing an issue on water.

JULIE: We thought that if the journal was organized thematically with each issue brought down to a single, elemental theme, the conversational aspects of this kind of publishing would be more evident. The water issue was planned for this past spring, but we held off for a number of reasons. I've found it an interesting position to be in— sitting with people's work on my desk for the entire summer and reading such beautiful and important writing about water, at the same time as we've been struggling financially to find ways to keep *The Peterborough Review* afloat.

DOUG: Shall we hear from Miigwewin-kwe?

WILMA: Traditionally, the Nishnaabeg have had a belief that water nourishes all of creation. It comes from the West, from the thunder-beings. Water is pure and sacred and cleansing. As well as being something physical to quench our thirsts, it helps us emotionally. Water has spirit. It is known to us as the veins which flow through

Mother Earth. All of the ponds, lakes, streams, oceans and seas are part of our Mother's body. For this reason, we give thanks for the veins of our Mother, the earth. It is the women who are the care-takers and carriers of that water. Our inheritance was to give birth to human beings, to spirit beings, through water. In traditional ways, as long as we have known, women are responsible for the water in ceremonies, to carry it and pray for it. We say that we speak with that water. In our ceremonies we sing for it. To me, my first thought about water is Nishnaabeg-kwe—the sacred life. Water can be wel-coming and helpful, but we can also see that it is powerful. It is one of the elements that has to be respected when we use it, or when it uses us. We know that if water runs for a long time, no matter how strong a rock is that water can shape that rock, water can move that rock. We have to know the water. As Nishnaabeg, we know when the water is safe, we know how to check the safety, we know where there are currents, where to go at what times … In a physical way, as a physical element, we can foresee its danger. A year and a half ago, my brother drowned in this lake, in March. The ice was safe when he travelled across from the island to the mainland. We assume he took the same route to try to get back to the cabin in the same day, but in the evening, it was not safe. I've come to understand since that time that it was because he was in a troubled time … it was like a welcoming, the water was opening up to him to come back. He was born by water, he was taken back to the Gzhwe Manidoo by the water. There is that part of water that is frightening because we can't survive under water like the fishes. But to me, the water has continued to be a very good thing…

ALICE: Julie, when you said that you were going to do the water issue in the spring—we believe that water is a life-giver from the West and the season of the West is the fall. So I think it's appropriate that we talk about the water now, in the autumn. We believe that Creation happened in four quarters, in the four directions. Each of the four directions has a life-giver: the east is food, south is sun, west is water and north is air. Without any one of those things, we wouldn't last long on this earth. We believe that water is a spirit. I remember once when we were having a sweat, a visiting Elder kept saying that this was a powerful place because he could feel the spirit of the water. I've always lived by the water, but I had never thought of it in that depth, as he explained it, in terms of spirit. We think of water, like Wilma says, as the life-blood of the Gzhwe Manidoo. We know of the vitalizing power of blood, and the role of water in our own blood. As women, when we carry our babies, it is throughout blood that we nourish the babies, feed the babies, give them drink. We think about all the rivers, the lakes, the streams, that are sacred to native peoples all over the world—the vitalizing power of the water, its cleansing nature. The Gzhwe Manidoo told us that we are to keep the water clean. If we keep the life-blood of the Great Mother clean, then she will keep us clean.

WINSTON: We take water for granted. I went out on a fast two years ago and couldn't have any water or food. I'm a heavy eater and thought I would have trouble when I didn't have any food. I didn't think I would have trouble with water—usually I might have a glass of water every six months. But after two days out in the bush, that's when you really think of how precious water is to Creation. You hear of our lakes and rivers being polluted … and we're in a crisis now that our hunting and fishing rights are being taken away from us. When the Gzhwe Manidoo sent us down here to live on Turtle Island, we were left to be the keepers of this land, to conserve the water and plant-life. I can remember when I was a small boy, my dad used to go fishing in a canoe—there were no motorboats. There was wild rice all over the place. You could paddle anywhere, throw your line in, and not catch a weed. Now the milfoil has just gone rampant. Today, that water that is so precious to the Nishnaabeg, for the fish, and for his means of putting food on his table, is being taken right from his mouth. The non-native society, those making money out there, feels that it is the Nishnaabeg taking all the fish away. Yet, the fish are being caught by sport fishermen who run around in the lakes and rivers in their big, fancy bass-boats, with fish finders. It's pretty bad when this is being taken away from us to satisfy their need. People don't want to buy cottages unless they are on the lakefront. Many of them don't have the right septic system, and they dump into the water. It's all turned around—it's always the Nishnaabeg who is at fault for draining the lakes.

DOUG: I think it is appropriate that the women spoke first because in our ceremonies, the women are asked to pray for the water, and tell stories about the water. We come onto the earth encased in water and it is a warmth that we remember. It nurtures. Water heals and it is free. When we are sad, when we have difficulty, when we are in pain, we cry. The tears that come through our eyes and drip down our cheeks—that's the healing process and to us, it is a natural gift that is given to us. In the womb, and from the day we step onto the earth, we have the ability to be healed by crying. Crying occurs when we want to feel comfort. We always associate comfort with the spirits—having that working. The spirits are doing their work when we cry, when we're in pain. There is pain, there is difficulty, there is struggle on this earth plane. There are forces here that work against good. Water helps us to deal with that. But at the same time as being a life-giver, water can take life away. Water can drown you, suffocate you. It has the power of moving mountains, it has the power of coming down on earth so fast that will cause floods. We have many stories of that in our history. There was once, way back beyond memory, a big flood here. Water went beyond the treetops and many people drowned and many animals were taken away. But through that struggle, we were able to retain many of our teachings. Water helped to remind us of our spirituality and it is still doing that. We are reminded that a lot of our very being, and our soul is water. We're very closely connected to it. It is something we cannot do without and we must hold it sacred. We must not desecrate it. We must drink it with care. Originally, it is said that The Great Spirit took some water and showed it to the Nishnaabeg and said: "This will be very important to you. This will keep you alive when nothing else will." I can see, as Winston is saying that we are drifting away. We are walking away from these sacred things. We see that every day when fast, noisy, powerful motorboats tear through that blood of Mother Earth—so unloving. It rips me apart to see that. Water is supposed to be free, but I was so thirsty the other day driving through a little town, that I bought water. I paid $1.39 for a bottle of water. I sat there, thinking about it, all the things I was taught, and thought, "My gosh!" It really hurt. We've twisted the whole thing around. To see something so sacred, so desecrated— it really bothered me.

ALICE: Water is the gift of the Gzhwe Manidoo. When you have to go and buy it, it is a horrible insult. It was given. It's like when Nishnaabeg were told about buying land. They said, "How can you buy land? How can we sell you land?" We can't sell you air. We can't sell you water."

WINSTON: There was a time when you could go out there with a dipper and drink right out of that lake. You didn't have to worry about whether there was any two-cycle oil in your cup or not.

WILMA: And about the fishing rights ... the right that we have to fish is inherited. It has nothing to do with signing a piece of paper. It has to do with what we inherited as a people. The only one that can take that right away is the one that we believe is the Great Spirit. As women, we will speak up. It is part of our responsibility to speak up and to do it in a good spiritual way—to speak for the spirit of the water, to speak for the men and our children.

ALICE: It's not something we can chop up and sell and make a profit on and oppress other people ... it's a free gift. We try to find different ways to express that so that dominant culture can understand it. The way they are handling it is to kill these gifts. There are First Nations people all over the world who try so hard to teach the real way to look at these gifts—that they are precious and sacred and life! We are all connected. If you kill one part of it, through desecrating it and polluting it, you kill us all. It's not one little river that's wrecked. How can we say these things so that it will be understood by the people who control it? *It's* not us who made acid rain. *It's* not us who spew the poisons from the factories, the pulp and paper mills, the mines so that the animals in the water can't live. Like Wilma says, we inherited this. We try to use words and concepts in the English language to reach dominant cultures so that they can understand that we're all in it together.

DOUG: It is said by our old people that all the lakes and the rivers were named by our first people, but the major rivers like the St. Lawrence, which is Kitchi-ziibi. That goes beyond memory. We've been here on Turtle Island, for thousands of years. Our elders say that Creation took a long time, it wasn't something that happened in six days. Kitchi-ziibi was always known as Kitchi-ziibi. If you look at it in this spiritual sense, it then has a personality. The St. Lawrence River is a being. I often wonder what Kitchi-ziibi thinks of its new name. Maybe I should go stand by it and ask.

JULIE: In Canadian historiography, there is the Laurentian Theory, which talk about the importance of the St. Lawrence for economy and settlement and so on—that Canada was settled by its waterways. The River is talked about as a point of entry, not as an entity. It was the only way in, and so it was important. As was the canoe....

DOUG: The rivers were our highways. They were our reference points on Turtle Island. Even the names here have been changed. Buckhorn Lake was not Buckhorn Lake. Chemong Lake, Stoney Lake … these are all foreign names given to beautiful lakes which were sustaining. They sustained our people for a long time. That's what our stories say.

WINSTON: There is a river up here between Buckhorn and Bobcaygeon. *It* used to be called Squaw River—that's what the white people called it. *It* wasn't until recently that a fuss was made over that, and it was changed back to what it was always called— Maskwaa River. Maskwaa in Ojibway is "Red". Years ago, when the Nishnaabeg used to paddle through there the red rock on the shore used to cast a red shadow on the river. The non-Natives came along and thought the Nishnaabeg were saying Squaw River so that's what they called it.

DOUG: When they changed it back, they asked of the Elders here— old Gladys. She told them what it had always been called. Squaw is so derogatory—it's absolutely insulting to us, insulting to the river, insulting to the sacred water.

WINSTON: My brother has a tape. They interviewed a few of the older fellows up here—they're gone now—and a lot of these rivers and towns had different names. The Otonabee was not Otonabee. It was all changed little bits over time.

ALICE: Look at the word Kawartha. This is called the Kawarthas— the Kawartha Lakes. People say it's a native name. But because it's the Michi Saagiig Nishnaabeg and Nishnaabeg who are here, it should be an Nishnaabeg word. In our language, we don't have "r" or the "th" sound. It's not our word. We wouldn't dream of saying Kawartha.

WINSTON: I've often wondered about this word "Canada." You see that commercial on TV where this Indian fellow and his tribe are talking to the white settlers. They were talking about going to their village the white people dint' really know what they were saying. I've often wondered if that Anihsinaabe was saying come to our villages. "Cantoneh?" Cantoneh means "Do you understand?" And then right away they said "This place is called Canada."

ALICE: It's interesting too, about the great river. In our language, that was called Kichi-ziibi. Yet all the different nations all over the world must have had, in their own language, the same phrase: "The Great River, The Sacred River". In Quebec, Chissasibi on the east shore of James Bay means "The Great River" in Cree. In our language, when we say great, we mean it in a very spiritual sense.

JULIE: What about the springs that used to run under the Petroglyphs?

WINSTON: We don't know what happened—they're just not there. We used to stand on the rock and hear the water running underneath it. I don't know if it's be re-routed or what...

DOUG: There's a basic principle that our people believe about anything sacred. If it is not used, it will be taken from us. You can apply that to almost anything. Look how polluted Kichi-ziibi is. It's leaving us. It's going to be destroyed. Someday that river is either going to turn to mud or its' going to dry up. You can say the same for the Petroglyphs. That is a very sacred site, in fact super-sacred. It's been desecrated so the spirits will leave. What you see there now is purely physical. It has lost its sacredness. We know that by the water leaving.

JULIE: And inside the building they've painted the petroglyphs?

ALICE: What?!

DOUG: They did that—with the black crayon. The school children did that a couple of years after they were found. The rock was a grey colour. It's turned black now because of the pollution, but traditionally that kind of rock was grey and if you pecked at it with another rock, it turned white. The paintings were white on grey and could be seen very well. What's happened now with the black crayon on the petroglyph, it's exactly opposite to what it was traditionally. Again, a desecration.

WINSTON: We went out there the other night, me and Wilma, and had a pipe ceremony. We just got into our ceremony and this noise came on. I couldn't believe it. I couldn't even hear myself praying. The air-conditioning came on—it was pitiful. It made my heart feel sad. They don't seem to realize how sacred it is. A long time ago, before the shelter was there, the petroglyphs were covered with moss. When the Nishnaabeg went to pray, they rolled the moss back, prayed and then covered it over and left. Now, you can see what's going on. It's being developed into a tourist trap. The road has been pulled up and resurfaced. The road has always been that way and now it's upgraded? The place has been desecrated enough. We can't make money on sacred ground. It can't happen.

DOUG: The interpretation centre, which is separate from the glass-covered site, cost $1.5 million. They asked for native input after it was done. They're not getting it. They would love more than anything to get an OK from us to develop that into a tourist/money-making proposition.

ALICE: Even as a cultural centre … we have a cultural centre and a library in Curve Lake and to me they are dead places. I think what is it that would make it alive … really alive? Not a tourist attraction or a place for rich people to come and see Indian stuff, or read about Indians. We don't want to read books about Indians, we want to live it. People make a place alive. You don't see Nishnaabeg going to libraries or museums or galleries. Dead places, full of dead things. Certainly books and art are exciting, but they don't have the same life as people do. And the thing about water, water holds so much life. Think of the fish, turtles—all these beings have their work to do. The Turtle, to Nishnaabeg is sacred. In our teachings, a turtle is a type of messenger. White men could never understand how communication happened among Nishnaabeg people. They coined the term "moccasin telegraph" because they didn't understand what was happening in another. We believe that the Turtle is the messenger and takes the news form one village to the next. A fly will come along to drink of the water and a fish will eat it and then a bird will swoop down and eat the fish. There is no end to the circle. Frogs, snakes, ... and the loons. The people managing the water have tunnel vision—they only see money. Right there, we see the lake go higher and higher in the spring. The height of the lake is controlled by the Trent Water System. Our here there is a marsh where the loons lay their eggs. They raise the water and drown out the nests. It happens every year—nothing changes. When are they going to smarten up? It affects the fish spawns. If women are the keepers of the water, then I think, "Who's going to listen to us?" In this society women aren't listened to, let alone native women.

WINSTON: With fishing. They say that the fish are depleted because of the Nishnaabeg fishing though the ice. You can count on these two hands the number of people from here who fish during the winter. The rest are non-Native. Doug and I were fishing down here last winter. The game wardens pulled up to us and asked if we were from Curve Lake. We showed them the id and asked them why they were harassing us. We told them there were a truckload of non-Natives around the island and they should go and see if that had status cards.

They said "We're not from around here. We don't know…" We told them to take a drive down there. They weren't of our sight for two minutes, turned around and drove off.

DOUG: We can't drink the water out of Buckhorn Lake anymore—that's only twenty years. The last five years, we haven't been able to swim in it. What's the next stage? Imagine. If we don't have water… These cities around here get their water form rivers. Lakefield is in deep trouble already with its water.

ALICE: You know, I was in grade three in Kenora when I learned about water purification. In those days, everything was so neat—Science, Social Studies … so every time we would open a new topic I was resolved to pay attention and try to understand. We talk about how a town like Kenora purifies its water. Me, as a little Indian kid sitting in an all-white school, already I had been taught that Indians are dirty people. I was listening to my teacher and reading my little science book and I couldn't believe what sewers were. I couldn't believe it, my mind was fresh then. I didn't come from a place that had sewers. So I learned that what they did was take the sewer water and purify it thought a series of steps that go in a circle. I was stunned. I thought surely I must be misunderstanding something. Now, here I am an adult, living in Curve Lake and I read about how Lakefield flushes its sewers into the river and Peterborough is drinking Lakefield's shit. And I just think, "Oh my God!"

Since Time Immemorial:
An Illustrated History of the Michi Saagiig Nishnaabeg Territory

Since Time Immemorial

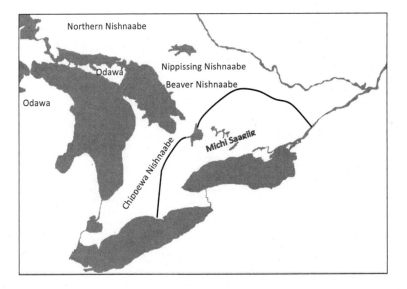

MAP I: Michi Saagiig traditional homelands. People tend to misunderstand how far back in time our people have lived on these lands.

Background map courtesy of L. Jackson and D. Clayton, Northeastern Archaeological Associates Ltd.

The Newcomers

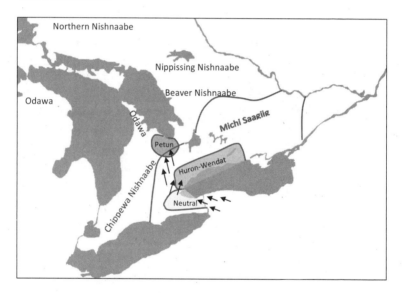

MAP 2: Approximately 800 A.D. Iroquoian speaking peoples move
into Michi Saagiig territory. It is recognized through a Wampum
diplomatic pact. The Michi Saagiig and Odawa alliance agree to let
these newcomers in and establish a corn-growing economy. They become
known as the Huron-Wendat, Neutral, and Petun. It was understood
that the territory was Michi Saagiig. We call the Huron-Wendat: people
who came from the south and lived in houses.

Background map courtesy of L. Jackson and D. Clayton, Northeastern Archaeological Associates Ltd.

The Relocation

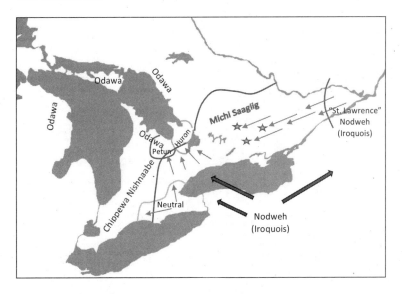

MAP 3: Approximately 1000 A.D., the Huron-Wendat, Petun and Neutrals ask if they may move further north to other locations on Michi Saagiig, Chippewa, and Odawa territory, further from the Nodweh to the south who were a threat. At this time the Iroquoian speaking people who lived on Gchi Ziibi (St. Lawrence) in the east also asked to come in to the territory.

Background map courtesy of L. Jackson and D. Clayton, Northeastern Archaeological Associates Ltd.

The 1650s

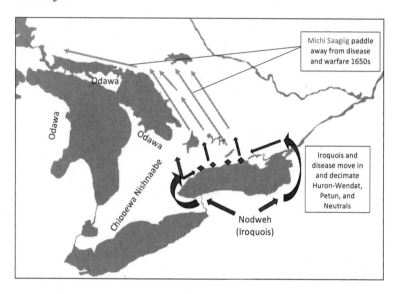

MAP 4: Disease and warfare have catastrophic effects on the Petun,
Neutral, and Huron-Wendat peoples who were almost totally
decimated and dispersed across the land. The Michi Saagiig temporarily
leave the area because of the diseases. They literally paddled away north.

Background map courtesy of L. Jackson and D. Clayton, Northeastern Archaeological Associates Ltd.

1670s: *The Return*

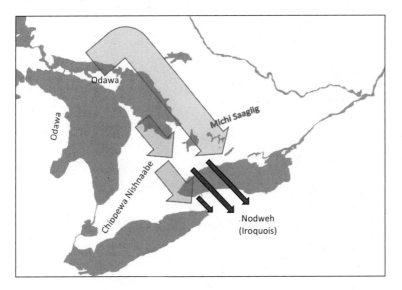

MAP 5: Approximately 20 years after leaving, the Michi Saagiig return to their traditional homelands south to the north shore of Lake Ontario where they find the Nodweh (Iroquois) people now living. With the help of the Odawa and Chippewa we pushed them out, back south of the Great Lakes.

Background map courtesy of L. Jackson and D. Clayton, Northeastern Archaeological Associates Ltd.

Michi Saagiig Today

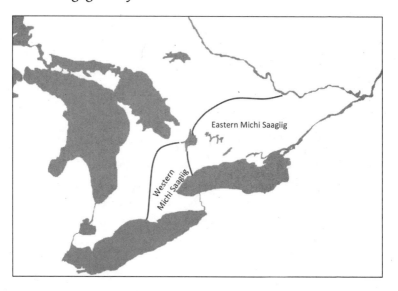

MAP 6: Today the Michi Saagiig are politically divided into eastern and western parts. The demarcation point between the two is the Toronto Portage, and not the Rouge Portage as believed by some. Peter Jones, an early Mississauga Missionary arbitrarily demarcated a boundary that erroneously overextended the eastern boundary to the Rouge River. My ancestors, from the eastern area travelled the Toronto Portage regularly.

Background map courtesy of L. Jackson and D. Clayton, Northeastern Archaeological Associates Ltd.

ACKNOWLEDGEMENTS

Chi'miigwech to a whole number of people who helped shape my Nishnaabeg Knowledge and took part in my upbringing: my grandmother Adeline, my mother Amelia, and my auntie Peggy. Chi'miigwech especially to Madden who is my grandmother's brother, and from whom I got much of the knowledge I convey in this book. A special thank you to his friend, James "Makoons" Taylor, and to Tom "Tinker" Taylor, with whom I spent much time on the land as a child.

Chi'miigwech to Leanne Betasamosake Simpson for recording, transcribing and editing these stories over the past several years, for finding funding for this project and for supporting this work through the publication process. Thank you to Julie Kapryka for recording, transcribing and editing the two Nokomis and the Shkin stories. Thanks to Todd Besant for his careful edits and to Madeline Whetung for her written feedback. Chi'miigwech to Elizabeth LaPensée for the cover art.

Chi'miigwech to another group of people whose help I cherish: my partner Christine Cairns, my children, Donna, Keesic, Saga, Sarah, and Kathleen, Alice Williams, Winston Taylor, Merritt Taylor, Mike Henry, Bill Fox, Paula Sherman, Christine Sy, Drew Hayden Taylor, Anne Taylor, Krista Coppaway, Brenda Maracle O'Toole, Dawn Lavalle Harvard and the staff at First Peoples House of Learning at Trent University, students throughout the years particularly Phil Abbott and Sarah Gauntlet, the staff at ARP Books, the Chief and Council of Curve Lake First Nation, and the Indigenous Arts Program of the Ontario Arts Council.

ENDNOTES

1 Eddie Benton, Migration Story in *Mishomis Book: The Voice of the Ojibway*, University of Minnesota Press, 2010.

2 I am not sure why the Chippewa'ag, Michi Saagiig Nishnaabeg and Nipissing get left out of this when it is talked about today.

3 There are many explanations for the Michi Saagiig Nishnaabeg word for Haudenosaunee people. According to Odawa Elder and language speaker Shirley Williams, it refers to the way they wore their hair. I remember our old people saying that it meant "people of the snake". Our word for the Michi Saagiig Nishnaabeg rattler is Chiwewe, and I think the "we" at the end of Naadawe refers to that snake. It could also refer to Haudenosaunee stories of a spirit with a head full of snakes. Basil Johnson, on page 14 of the *Anishinaubae Thesaurus* takes a literal approach and indicates that it means "They Who Fetch."

4 My great uncle is Madden Taylor and his friend is Makoons.

5 Petun are known as Tionantati in their own language and they are also known as the Tobacco people.

6 *Valley of the Trent* by Edwin Gillet, 1957, Champlain Society, Toronto, ON.

7 Minutes of the meeting of 1840, available through New Credit First Nation. Presented at the Mississauga Historical Conference in New Credit First Nation, February, 2012.

8 Minutes of the meeting of 1840, available through New Credit First Nation. Presented at the Mississauga Historical Conference in New Credit First Nation, February, 2012.

9 This was previously published in the Curve Lake Newsletter, June, 2011.

10 Whitcher and Venning qtd. in Guillet, Edwin C. 1969[1933]. Early Life in Upper Canada. Toronto: University of Toronto Press, 1969[1933], 268.

11 Guillet, Edwin C. 1969[1933]. Early Life in Upper Canada. Toronto: University of Toronto Press, 271-2. Emphasis added.

12 A previous version of this chapter was printed in the *Peterborough Review*, Volume 1, Number 1, 1994, Peterborough, ON, 43-47.

13 Blanket Diseases are small pox.

14 A previous version of this chapter was published in the *Peterborough Review*, Volume 1, number 2, 1994, 35-40.

15 Basic Call to Consciousness, Akwesasne Notes, 1977.

16 A previous version of this chapter was printed in the *Peterborough Review*, Volume 1, number 4, 38-47.

DOUG WILLIAMS (Gidigaa Migizi) is Anishinaabe and former Chief of Mississauga's Curve Lake First Nation. He is currently Co Director and Graduate Faculty for the Indigenous Studies Ph.D. Program at Trent University and oversees the cultural and spiritual component of the program. He is a member of the Pike Clan, and was one of the first graduates of what is now called Indigenous Studies at Trent University in 1972. He is a Pipe Carrier, Sweat Lodge Keeper, and ceremony leader. He is a language speaker and considers himself a trapper, a hunter and a fisher. Beyond his work in the academy, he is active at the community level and works to ensure that Indigenous Knowledge is maintained within the community.